ONE

DISCOVERING THE TRUE NATURE OF THE UNIVERSAL ACCORD

EZEKIAH

Through- Michelle LaVigne-Wedel

Write to **Print**

P.O. Box 1862
Merrimack, NH 03054
www.writetoprint.com

Copyright © 2003 by Write to Print and Michelle & Paul Wedel. All rights reserved. No part of this book may be reproduced in any form or by any electronic or mechanical means including information and retrieval systems, websites or Internet without permission from the publisher in writing.

Library of Congress Control Number: 2004100433

Ezekiah
One: Discovering The True Nature of the Universal Accord

ISBN 0-9745434-4-6

ORIGINAL COVER DESIGN: The Electric Wigwam

Editor: Paul Wedel

Printed in the United States of America

Address all inquiries to:

Write to Print
P.O. Box 1862
Merrimack, NH 03054
USA

URL: http:// www.writetoprint.com
E-mail: info@writetoprint.com

CHAPTER ONE
A BRIEF INTRODUCTION

Greetings from we who are here, beyond the vision of some, but always within your reach. I am Ezekiah. Though this is only one of many names I have answered to in my days upon your Earth. Now my state of being is not of the body. I sit with the teachers who are above and around you. I am what some would call a guiding voice. Indeed, this is my intention.

Why do I, and those like me, offer our services to you? Why should we attempt any intervention whatsoever into a predicament you have — from a higher state of consciousness — placed yourself into of your own free will?

One: Discovering the True Nature of The Universal Accord

The answer is simple. Because you have asked us to. Had you not asked, no assistance would be offered.

The density of the physical world binds to your flesh and your perceptions are thus limited by this restriction. These restrictions are not truly encumbering if you understand what they are and how to overcome or circumvent them.

In my most recent life on Earth, I was a man. I was a holy man who was visited by the power of the spirit in my life, as you yourself have been visited. The power of the ***Creator that is All*** changed my life. We are changed to the extent our understanding and ability allow us at the time of this visitation.

Who am I that I could teach you? I am nothing more than you. Only my placement in the order of the Universe allows me a wider view of perception that you may benefit from if you choose.

There is a natural order to each life-cycle everyone of us experiences. Each cycle has a purpose and goal we strive to achieve. Not an easy task, as we are asked

A Brief Introduction

to achieve this objective often with little or no mindful knowledge of what the ultimate goal is. It is, as some of you know too well, like walking a path through the woods in the dark of night.

When walking through the darkness, we must learn to develop other senses to make it through the woods without incident. So it is in walking through the path of your life's purpose. The senses you use to direct your life today as you search for your path to God may prove to be useless in finding your way to the One. To develop new senses that will wake you to the Unity of God, and to open your connection to the network of the Universal Accord, of which you are a component, is the true effort — the true light in the forest of the night.

CHAPTER TWO
COUNTING DOWN: THREE

When you hear the number three, you may think of many common phrases and objects. Some of the more common include the way we give a baseball batter three strikes before he is out of the game. It is unlucky to light three cigarettes from one match. There are three phases to Earth time — past, present and future. Children's stories often have three characters — for example; The Three Little Pigs.

We learn much from the mathematical soundness of triangles. Yet, all these examples are simple and basic. Although some of the most simple examples of **Three** we are familiar with hold much greater meaning, they are, for the most part, not an important implement in our search to reach **One**.

Three is the signifier of the divine mysteries. There are many divine mysteries in place around you. You may succeed in comprehending any or all of these mysteries to the extent that you begin to feel you have mastered the concepts. The true nature of the unity in any of these examples of **Three**, is merely a mirror of the greater impression of each divine mystery.

Our bodies have three parts, our physical, our intellectual and our spiritual — body, mind and soul. The joining of these three parts of each person into a complete being is the first of the divine mysteries. The order of creation that separated the energy that is your greater self into these three unique, yet unified portions of your being is a force that is hard to put into words, and must be felt to be understood.

Our life-cycle is the most simple of these divine mysteries. All living things are born, grow, then die. Just as a story has a beginning, a middle, and an end. It is the nature of living things to come into being, grow through a pattern of learning, and then come to an end. Even the families we are born into become, grow, and then end. The very construction of the family is, when properly pieced together, an example of *Three*. The father, the mother, the child (or children).

Our goal in life, as we reach for **One** can be considered a divine mystery of **Three**. For our goal is more than just in this physical life. Your journey to reach **One** continues in the three different stages of your consciousness' existence. Throughout all these stages, you continue on your one solid goal, even when the path is lost to your eyes.

The first stage is that which you came from. That is the spirits, souls and consciousnesses that choose to maintain an identity when they are no longer in a physical body in order to retain their search for **One**. It is notable to mention that just because a being is not in a physical body does not assure that the being has evolved spiritually.

Counting Down: Three

In the non-physical, a personality continues to grow and learn. It may interact with other beings who have returned to the non-physical.

If it can master the understanding of what it means to be **One**, it may choose not to return to the physical. But more often than not, beings need more practice in the lessons that are available only in the physical plane, so they leave the realms of pure life-force and return to a physical body in order to learn.

Childhood of physical life is the second part of this particular divine mystery of **Three**.

The child is fresh, new, and untainted — not an easy task when you consider that every child is truly a very old soul with a considerable, even immeasurable, total sum of knowledge. A child's work is to play, learning the most simple of lessons through exploration and innocence. The child phase allows the old, experienced soul to find a new start, to practice and reinforce the largely straightforward lessons that made up the essential foundation of all things to be learned and experienced in the next phase.

The child phase allows a master to once again be a student. Without reservation, without pride, without hesitation, the child phase brings each personality, regardless of the position in the spirit phase, back to a ground point.

The third and last phase of this divine mystery is the time you become aware of the recommencement towards your goal. This resumption can be very different for each individual personality. Often seen as an event or moment in time, for some it will be sudden and life changing. For others it could happen in stages, each stage bringing a bit more power or meaning to the individual's life and understanding. For some, it will seep in slowly overtime, in a manner that will make the change imperceptible. For others, this time could be so perverted by circumstances, that it is perceived not as a positive movement or experience, but rather as a trauma or loss of innocence.

This is the moment we find ourselves questioning our faith, understanding our own humanity, and realizing our immortality. It may be as violent as a near-death experience, or as passive as a pleasant dream. For some, it is simply a thought that is not there one moment, but is there the next. But for each, it happens and signifies the end of the child phase, regardless if the individual is 10 or 100 years old.

I would not be surprised if you know the year, date, perhaps even the exact time of day when you entered this phase — the moment you realized that your body was not going to live forever — the moment you realized that God was not a church — the moment you realized that you were an eternal being.

The next divine mystery of **Three** concerns our cycles in our behavior while we live on the Earth. Each and every one of us plays roles. Like the triangle, each side holds up the others and makes it possible for the whole to exist. Each and every one of us is, at any given time, either a Savior, a Victim, or a Perpetrator.

This cycle is ongoing. Today you may be a victim, tomorrow you may be the perpetrator of harm on another, tomorrow you may save someone from harm. Overall, your life may have the ring and tone of any of these three stages. Each of these stages has their lessons. Each has a purpose and a payment. And though you might think the roll of the savior is always beneficial over that of the victim, lessons from any one of these stages are equally important.

The balance between these three sides is necessary. To be a perpetrator is not to say that you are being evil in all cases. We can all inflict harm on another without knowing it, or more accurately, without wanting to know it. But without perpetrators, there would be no victims; and without victims, there would be no saviors. In order for you to gain the positive benefits of being the redeemer and teacher, you must have someone to help, teach or otherwise save. This juxtaposition of forces is the core of this divine mystery.

Returning to the analogy of the sides of the triangle being each of these stages — victim, savior, and perpetrator — we must realize that they are boundaries. Inside the triangle exists the heart of the shape, just as inside this cycle exists the heart of the truth of **Three.**

Another divine mystery of **Three** concerns the way mankind perceives God.

Almost all major religions have a concept of God that has three parts. For example, regardless of the fact that Christians profess the belief in one God (the **One** concept in simple form), their concept is actually of three gods united as one. The Christian Holy Trinity consisting of the Father, Son, and Holy Ghost is actually the concept of **Three**, not **One**. The Holy Trinity as a mode of **Three** is plainly another form of the "Spiritual head and three pillars" of the Jewish Kabala.

Another divine mystery of **Three** relates to what could be called forces of actions. Everything in action, whether that action is of a physical or unworldly nature has three forces that are always putting pressure on it in order to affect it.

The first of these forces of action could be called the rigid force, or some know it as the passive force. It is the force that keeps an object or moment going forward in the current direction. Its influence is to make something continue as it is. This force is a moving force that maintains the momentum of the thing itself in the exact way in which it is evolving.

The second force of action could be called the adapting force or active force. This force works to change the object or direction. This force gives resistance and pushes the direction of an object or concept to change. Often in direct opposition to the original direction, it could easily be misinterpreted as a negative force. On the contrary, more often than not, this force is the force of change and growth.

The third force of action could be called indifference or neutral action. This may not seem like a force, but it is unquestionably the most dangerous of the three. This force does not affect an object or concept to move forward or change direction. It encourages it to stop, become void, and die. Under certain conditions, this force can be quite destructive. It can stop evolution of the object or idea in its tracks, not allowing it to move forward or onto another course. Regardless of the danger of this pitfall, the force of neutral action is the most important of all. Without it, there would be no common ground for the rigid force and the adaptive to unite.

Counting Down: Three

There are many examples of **Three** in place around you. Some other examples may not be divine mysteries, but are nevertheless interesting and useful.

The harmony of **Three** can be seen in music. The major chords in each scale are a combination of three perfect tones. A chair or table must have at least three legs or feet in order to stand on its own. Most people have three parts to their daily routine — work or school, home time, sleep. Your health consists of your physical, emotional, and social well being. Your body needs food, water, and rest to live. Your spirit needs hope, trust, and purpose. Your soul needs love, compassion and companionship.

We are comfortable with the number three. And this is how it should be. Three is the number of balance. Everything that is a representation of the concept of **Three** will be in balance if it is being applied correctly. Balance is the most important aspect of **Three**.

Picture three objects attached to a string. Two are attached to opposite sides of a string. These two are the rigid and adaptive; positive and negative; or active and passive elements. Another is attached to the center of the string. Now, picture yourself holding the center ball — the neutral influence. From it, the string will hang down equally on both sides, creating a balance between the two opposite ends. Hold the string in any other place or hold any of the other balls and the thing would not be balanced.

The balance of **Three** is imperative. All the examples of **Three** in your life need to be in perfect balance for you to be healthy, happy, and productive. Your soul knows this and is in constant flux as it tries to adjust the different balances of the many examples of **Three** you are exposed to. Ultimately, your ability to realize your spiritual goals is based largely on your ability to balance the many manifestations of **Three** in your life.

If your balance is too far in any direction, you would be in trouble. This is especially true if you fail to recognize the concept of **Three** involved in your situation at all. Most everything you are occupied with in your life, no matter what the nature of it, will aptly be a demonstration of **Three** in some form. To comprehend this, define the **Three** that is in action and then to find the point of balance will bring the problem into the open and help you to find a solution to your problem — a balance.

CHAPTER THREE
LIVING IN THREE

The balance of **Three** is important in each of our lives. Even those of us who are not in a body have our own balances of **Three** we must maintain. Some of these concern our work to maintain a balance in our own individual spiritual work, help you with your spiritual quest, and maintain our communal spiritual quest as a unified collective of spiritual beings.

Even in this state, far beyond the human condition, there are still struggles to maintain a balance. Balance is not assured for any being who is still subjected to the pulls and influences of a personality they maintain in order to communicate with humans.

Before you can start to live in **Three** and keep it in balance, you have to discover the hidden — and not so hidden — **Threes** in your life. If you find one or two, you're not looking hard enough. If you find five or ten, keep trying. If you find that just about everything in your life is a form of **Three**, you are finally seeing the big picture. Everything in your physical life is somehow affected by the concept of **Three**. There are very few exceptions.

When you are trying to balance these aspects of your life there are a few things you need to know right from the onset. Balance doesn't mean equal in all cases.

Lets look back at the example of the object we spoke about in the previous chapter; the object made of string and three balls. If one of the end balls is heavier than the other, when you hold the interior ball in the direct center of the string the object would be far from balanced. Being balanced and being centered, in this case, are not the same. That is why the first thing to remember when living in **Three** is that the middle ground is not always good ground.

In fact, middle ground is almost always the worst place to be. Remember the danger of neutral force. With the middle ground comes the risk of apathy, indecision, and stagnation.

The pitfalls of middle ground can be disguised in many different ways. It can look like a lack of interest. It can be hiding in a feeling of helplessness. It can even appear to be a sense of satisfaction that tricks you into believing you have completed your growth, and don't have to keep striving forward.

Speaking of this artificial sense of satisfaction created by the neutral point, it is important to point out how often this happens and how many people fall into the trap when it comes to the most important of spiritual issues. Eventually, the unlucky individuals who fall into this trap, find themselves on the other side of the veil between physical life and what could be called the afterlife, looking back at what they did while they were in their body and thinking, "How could I have been so blind!"

All the while, regretting leaning on their laurels rather than getting back to work.

How could these beings, who are really masters — indeed Gods — been so blind? How could you and those around you, who are really masters — indeed Gods — be so blind? The answer can be seen in the following example:

It is common knowledge that we are currently living in what we can call the end-times. The time of the ascension of souls is soon to take place. This is not a myth. This is not a story. This is a fact. No matter if you call this the time of the Apocalypse, Revelation, Rapture, or Ascension, (which is what I choose to call it), the whole of the earth is on the brink of change. I am not telling you anything new with this information, I'm sure. You know this.

Think about your concept of the Ascension and what will happen, and we will look at the **Three** involved in this information and how you might be treading on dangerous middle ground.

For those of you who might not know about the Ascension, it is, in a nutshell, a time heralded by the return of the Christ, or Christ energy to the Earth. In other words, it is the time when the Earth will be changed — transformed — reborn. Depending on which belief system you are currently engaged in, your perspective of the Ascension and the way it will unfold will vary from believing the being known as Jesus Christ will return to the Earth in physical form, to believing that the energy of the Earth itself will take over.

It does not matter what you believe the catalyst is for the purpose of this example. It doesn't matter if you believe that this great change will come on the wings of Angels or on the tails of flying saucers, so long as you are aware that it is coming — and coming soon.

There are several examples of **Three** that come into play when we talk about the coming age of man — the end-times. The one I would like to explore has the most dangerous pitfall hidden in its middle ground. It is the **Three** formed on all sides by human understanding of the process, human fear of what will happen, and human acquiescence of the whole situation.

Any who have studied, read about or even pondered what could be called the apocalypse are familiar with what the world will be like after the time of tribulations and the Earth is renewed. Life will be once again as it should be. There will be a simplicity to life that has been missing from human existence for too long. There will be a balance. Everyone will be in harmony with everyone else. There will be no sickness or evil. There will be a true utopia, where the love of God will fill all, and all will be right with the world.

What do we believe we know about the time before the renewal of Earth? What do we know about the time of tribulations? Many things. It has been recorded in the prophecy of many holy books that before the actual time when the Earth settles back to a peaceful state, many horrible and almost unspeakable things may happen.

Yet, as with all prophecy, there is always a glimmer of hope that this terrible future can be averted. If human-kind takes heed and changes their ways, things can be different.

One: Discovering the True Nature of The Universal Accord

Herein lies the **Three**. The first part is moving toward the future of tribulations; part two is the changing of direction and moving away from the future of tribulations; and, of course, the third part is muddy middle ground of inaction and simply not caring.

The path mankind is now traveling is clearly the movement towards destruction. The focus of the energy encompassed in this **Three** is that which compels a thing to keep moving in the same direction — in this case the direction is grim.

The proof of this can be seen all around you. What you would call natural disasters — but we call natural progressions — have already started to happen, and will only continue to become greater in proportion and frequency.

Earthquakes of 7 or more on the rictor scale were once unheard of, but are now happening with some regularity.

If the path is not adjusted by the balancing of the aspects of this **Three**, earthquakes of this magnitude will continue, and get stronger. In a few years from this writing, earthquakes greater than 10 on the rictor scale may be happening in areas which are prone to quakes now. In addition to that, earthquakes of 7 and 8 points will be considered no more out of the ordinary in those areas than a 4 or 5 point earthquake is today. Places where earthquakes are rare will begin to have them. Oceans will start to open up with subterranean volcanic activity on such a scale, that tidal waves and tsunamis will make living by the ocean precariously foolish, and eventually impossible.

Volcanic activity on land will also increase. Over the next few years we will likely see more and more dormant volcanoes begin to come back to life. As they do, large sink holes will form in places where once solid material far below the surface melts and flows away. In other places, large mounds will appear as pools of this newly melted magma well up, creating new volcanic hot spots, and in some cases, open pits of volcanic emissions, including all the deadly gases produced by these reactions. The skies will be blackened by the ash. Day and night will be all the same. Cold will set in, and summer and winter will be all the same. The changing of the natural ecosystem will kill many of the world's animal species.

If this **Three** is not put into balance, the magnitude of the natural disasters will continue to grow. One by one, the Earth's shaking will cause catastrophic failures of nuclear power plants and weapons facilities. Chemical weapons and waste facilities across the globe will simply crack open under the stress and their man-made poison will be free to spread into the air, water, and food supply. War will rage across the face of the earth as nations struggle over the quickly dwindling resources they need to keep themselves alive.

This scenario of gloom and doom is one that many people believe we cannot avoid. After all, they see it beginning around them in the form of increased volcanic and seismic activity, as well as super germs resistant to conventional medicines, and more.

In truth, there is a way to avoid this bleak future. Although I would be remiss to leave the reader with the suggestion that it will be easy. The odds are against it, in a two to one ratio. This is because of the different aspects of the **Three** involved. Only one can lead to an non-violent future, and easy transition for humans and the world we live on.

If we do not change our path, we are surely going to face this future. If we do nothing, and stay in the muddy middle ground of apathy, not even making the effort to acknowledge the changes ahead of us, we do more than just condemn ourselves to facing a future of dreadfulness. By doing nothing and sticking in this muddy middle ground of apathy, we relinquish our power to create our own future.

By not caring, we allow those who have an opinion to create what they wish for all of us. Unfortunately, because of centuries of conditioning from religious teachings, and the saturation of the public with disparaging information via apocalyptical preachers, the media, and the Internet, the focus of the overall consensus of the people is that the future is hopeless.

The Earth is going to change and grow regardless of what happens to the people on her. It does not matter to the evolution of the Earth if humans endure trials, or transition with minimal strife. All aspects of this **Three** will eventually bring people to the other side. That is certain. It is simply how they choose to get there that is in question.

The only focus of this **Three** that gives hope to the possibility of a peaceful passage is that of change. Change can only come if people are aware of the reality of the change, and are not afraid of it. This is a difficult task. To know that you are, in all probability, facing a terrifying time of physical trials and suffering that could take your mortal life and yet to not be afraid is too much for many teachers to ask of their students.

That is why your spirit guides, guardian angels, and teachers are prepared and revved up into high gear in order to feed you as much information as you can handle or want in this time so that you can prepare yourself. Only through preparation for the worse, can you find some sense of security without totally ignoring the possibility.

Only by being prepared for the worse, can you give your energy to assist in balancing this **Three**, with an emphasis on personal power, and not on fear or apathy.

Some of you already know this, even if you never thought about it in your conscious state. Many of you may have a strong feeling to live in a certain area. You may have been inspired to collect water and food in a safe place. You may have drawn up plans for contacting your loved ones if these changes cut you off from each other. These are all good things you are being encouraged to do. Moreover, and more important in many cases, you need to prepare spiritually and emotionally for the troubles the future could hold.

If you are prepared both physically and spiritually for what could be, you are taking weight away from the force that is moving forward to this horrific future. If you are prepared, you are adding your energy to that direction that will bring change! And if enough people make the effort to prepare, the energies applied to this **Three** will shift and change will happen.

Once you feel prepared, beware you do not fall into the trap of middle ground. If once you are prepared, you feel so confident in your safety that you come to disregard your knowledge of how hard it will get, then you become a victim of the inaction of the neutral. You say, "I am prepared and thus I am safe." Then you will do nothing more.

It is true, that over time, you may have accumulated so much in the way of physical goods that you need nothing else to survive a great catastrophe. However, there is always room for you to continue with preparations of your spirit and soul. The work on yourself will never end.

If you allow inaction to stop you from making the necessary spiritual preparations, you will be stuck in middle ground. Thus giving your vote for the structure of the future to another. It is important that you keep your works and words to others compassionate. You must find the strength to forgive those who have crossed you. You must find and share the Christed energy inside of yourself. Most of all, you must focus on the optimistic.

I know in times of trouble, it is difficult to focus on the optimistic. When the Earth begins to shake under your feet, you are likely to be filled with fear, not with

Living In Three

positive thoughts. This is why you must prepare. Be ready, so when the Earth shakes, you will know you are going to survive. You may be afraid of the change itself, but you will not fear for your mortality and for the lives of those you love.

Remember, because the balance of the energy of this **Three** is all important to the outcome of the future, there is an inherent "catch 22" in this situation. That is, if you do not assume you are safe and thus work hard to prepare, in all likelihood you will be safe.

If you prepare yourself, physically and spiritually, you will be moving in a direction that will create the energy of survival around you. Your will to survive and succeed will empower you to do just that. Your work toward being spiritually ready for the moment, will help you expand yourself and grow in a sacred way that can only assist you in this process.

The overall consensus of the human souls all focused on spiritual transitioning through the foundation of sound preparation of soul and body can affect the form of the transition. This means, if all people applied the effort to be spiritually and physically prepared for the tribulations of the end-time, the very nature of the end-times would be affected and the horrors that could beset the world would not have to happen at all. The Earth would transition in a quiet, peaceful manner.

Even if the overall future of the Earth changes are grim, if you work on your own situation, then in the corner of the globe where you reside the story can be different. If enough like-minded and focused people work on preparing their bodies and souls for these changes, they could create a microcosm of relative safety in a localized area. For that matter, even a few individuals, just one or two, could create a safe zone around themselves if they prepare themselves for the worse.

Unfortunately, the false sense of safety created by the neutral phase has far too many people fooled into inaction. To allow yourself to fall into the pitfall of inaction is to, beyond a doubt, condemn your body to death and your soul to moving on, away from the new Earth you long for — like Moses, never to enter the promised land he dreamed of.

The above is a stark example of what can happen when the balance of **Three** is missing from any given situation. It was not meant to scare you. I chose it as a word to the wise, to remind you that success is not a promise, it is a reward.

Another example of what can happen when **Three** is not in balance concerns another issue you are likely to face in your spiritual growth. This is one where the neutral middle road is probably the more wise choice for you to take, though you are, in all probability, not prone to choose the neutral position.

When you start on a spiritual path, you experience wonderful things. Enlightenment comes to you. Energy of the spirit brightens you and makes you come alive. Whether your path of choice is traditional or obscure; regardless if you belong to an organized religion or make your own interpretation of the facts around you, you will experience energy, a sense of fulfillment, and a satisfaction in proportion to the effort you put into your convictions.

Each path is unique. Even people who gather together in the same building and follow the same book of dogma will have a personal and totally individual rapport with God. Paths are always different, but the ending point is always the same if the path is a good one. Not all paths are.

Good or not, each person's path is their own incontrovertible choice. No one has the right or the duty to force a change in the path of another. Even if you believe that someone you love is heading for total spiritual ruin, you have no right to force your ways upon them. Herein lies the **Three**.

The **Three** in this situation comes into play as we move forward on our own chosen spiritual course. As we do, we feel the power, the energy, the fulfillment our chosen faith brings to us. We love our spiritual direction and we find it hard to understand that anyone could not understand or could disagree with what is so plainly the unquestionable truth to us. Just like it is hard to imagine that someone could despise your favorite song or detest your most loved food, it is very difficult for people to accept the fact that someone else may see little or no value in a way of life they see and feel as divine.

The elements of **Three** in this case would be your belief and faith in your own path, respect for the paths of others, and acceptance of other ways and beliefs.

Far too often, people are so excited about their way that they fail to realize that their way is not the only way. They fail to see that the ways of others around them could be just as valid, maybe even more so.

For example, people who classify themselves as Christians often are deluded by the imbalance of this action of **Three** into believing that only those who accept the man Jesus Christ as a Savior will attain heaven. To the exact opposite, people of the Buddhist religion do not even believe in a "God" figure and believe that the worship of Jesus Christ can distract one from attainment of perfection. By naming Christians and Buddhists, I am by no means saying these are the only people who are guilty of this distortion, or that any individual who considers himself Buddhist or Christian makes this mistake.

In fact, almost all organized religions and faiths, even those who profess to be accepting of others, are at the very best, tolerant of others views, but remain critical of the other's belief systems and steadfast in the conviction that the others' beliefs are wrong and destined to damnation.

This is a dangerous position to take. Not only could you be missing out on a piece of the truth that the other may hold that you don't have, but you also darken your soul with a deep form of prejudice. This prejudice will cause you spiritual harm, if nothing else.

If your balance is too far a skewed, your sense of prejudice may evolve into a hidden hatred. If it does, you may not know it. Don't expect to see yourself showing signs of outward hatred. The symptoms of this hidden hatred manifest themselves in subtle ways. People who harbor this hidden hatred, show it by being overly pious of their own belief. They are far too righteous concerning their own viewpoint. They are condescending to others and believe only they and those who they see as contemporaries have a clue as to what is truly going on.

Hidden hatred is the downfall of more than one well-informed person. To know the truth is not enough if you don't know how to balance the concept of **Three**.

Many people believe it is their mission in this life to evangelize about their belief systems. It is a sound belief, so long as it is done with the balance of **Three** in mind. That is, your knowledge is there for all to share in — *if they choose*. Never forget those last few words. The choice of the person you are sharing with must be respected above everything else.

The other active direction you can take out of balance with this phase of **Three** is when you are so open to everyone's belief that you cannot find your own path. To believe in everything is not just as bad, but is actually worse than believing in nothing at all. How can anyone hope to reach the end of their journey if they keep taking side roads along the way. How can you hope to find your spiritual goal if you keep getting distracted by the words and belief of those around you.

Just as you have to accept that everyone else's beliefs could be right and could lead to the same place you believe you are going — just as you must accept their right to follow their own path, and not force them to change — you must also understand that just because their path is right for them, it may not be right for you. Just because they use endless words of reason and countless quotes from dogma, and fully believe in their path, it does not mean the path is correct for you.

Often, people fall into the pitfall that to have an open and accepting mind means they have to try everything, accept everything, and believe everything. This is not true.

So, when considering everything we just discussed in the context of **Three**, we see that there are dangerous pitfalls in both the active directions. That is why, in this example, it is better to choose a common ground. Choosing common ground is the exception, not the rule.

The common ground in this situation would be to hold strongly in your path and belief. Share your belief when you see fit, but do not expect others to change their path for you. Likewise, do not change your path at the insistence of others, even if they seem to be moving faster to the goal.

Living In Three

It has been said in the Bible, lukewarm is not good; and it is so. In most cases, to be fired up about an issue or idea is better than to not care. To have an opinion, even if other's think that opinion is wrong, is better than not to think. To move in a direction is better than to stand still in almost all cases.

This can be applied in a practical matter around your life. Perhaps you work in a company, day after day, doing the same old job. You feel your life is in a rut. You don't see any future for yourself. Maybe you are even counting the days until you can retire, even if those days are in the thousands! You're not happy, though you may be comfortable. You may not be joyful at the thought of Monday coming around, but at least you know the routine. You may wish you had a better job, but at least you don't have to have your interview suit dry cleaned and get your résumé updated. You are dead in your tracks, and every emotion from your higher self knows it and screams for movement. Yet your greed tells you that you're making money and that's good. Your fear tells you that you are secure and that's good, and your laziness tells you that lack of movement means less work, trouble, and stress, and that's good too. So, your greed, fear, and laziness win out. You stay in that rut you are not happy with.

You could argue that you have better reasons to stay where you are not happy. You say you can't make a change, even for your own happiness, because you have too many obligations, there are no better jobs out there, or you are not ready for the move. But what is really going on is that at least one or more of your concepts of **Three** surrounding your job is warped and off balance.

Remember the sacred mystery of **Three** in the cycle of Savior, Victim, and Perpetrator we went over in the last chapter? This cycle is the first and most obvious one that is out of balance.

Clever as people are, they find the most interesting ways to warp this balance. When a person says they have to say in the job they are in, even though they don't like the work and they are not happy, claiming reasons like, "I have to pay my bills somehow; I have kids to feed;" or "Without me the company would go down the tubes. Only I know how to run that computer." or

Living In Three

any other such excuse, they are really being all three: Savior, Victim, and Perpetrator.

They see themselves as a Savior, in that without their pain and suffering at this job they don't like, others would be made to endure hardships. Without their unwavering misery, the children would starve, the car would be repossessed or the company would go bankrupt. They become an instant Savior. Not just any redeemer, but one who must relinquish their rights to happiness for others.

Unflattering as it is to say, they have fooled themselves into believing that being in unbalanced middle ground means they are selfless and Christed. They — even without knowing what terms or words to use to express their attitude — perceive themselves sacrificing their happiness for others, like they are selfless examples of Christ energy. They feel noble for their sacrifice. Their sense of sacrifice makes them feel like they have some value they can focus on, rather than to see their own lack of momentum and ambition to better their situation.

Nevertheless, as a Savior, they are never truly happy. This is because even if they cannot admit it to themselves, their higher, more seeing soul knows that they are not really saving anyone. Yes, they may pay the bills with that job, but they could find a way to pay the bills and still be happy themselves if they did not get stuck in the muck of muddy middle ground.

In addition to being a Savior, they are also the victim. They convince themselves that they must suffer for others. They must endure this humdrum job that is stagnation in employment form in order to take care of someone else. They are miserable inside themselves. They are unhappy and make those around them unhappy. They refuse to see and escape from their victim-hood not because they could not see it if they tried, but because they want to believe that they are the uncomplaining, long suffering, good hearted Christ energy.

Being in unbalanced middle ground, they are not motivated to stop being a victim and get on with the purpose of their life. Instead, they slip into the belief that being a victim *is* the purpose of their life.

More than just being the savior and victim, people in this situation are also, if not predominantly, the perpetrator. They inflict all this pain and suffering on themselves. It is their own imbalance that forces them to be the victim. They create the hurt that surrounds them. They choose the unmoving and inaction of neutral ground. They fool themselves into believing that they are helpless to change it. Their laziness makes them feel too tired or weak to try. Their fear makes them feel too insecure to make that leap of faith people so often need to break out of the treacherous trap of neutral ground.

If the balance of this cycle of **Three** were to return, the people who find themselves in this situation would know that they were free to succeed in being happy. They would begin to move in the direction that would bring them to a place where they were happy. If that place was in the same job, so be it. If it were in another job, that is fine, too. Where they are happy is not as important as that they are happy.

By putting the amount of victim roll they are willing to play in perspective, they will release themselves from a huge amount of obligation without loosing personal responsibility for those matters. They will no longer find the act of bringing home money to feed their children so terribly burdening. Instead, they will feel a pride in supporting their dependents. The fear of failure will turn into the pleasure of accomplishment

If you balance the victim from the equation, you also balance the perpetrator, because the two are inseparable. Because all the aspects of any **Three** are associated, that means that the greater of the balance, and thus the proper side to be on is that of the Savior — but not the Savior of your family, rather, the savior of yourself. When you put yourself into a position where you are happy and able to grow, you have become your own Savior, your own personal Christ. In other words, you have become Christed in this circumstance.

To be balanced is to be Christed. To be Christed allows you to be aware of your true relationship and bond to the Universal Accord that you are part of.

Just about all circumstances and events in a person's life gives them the opportunity to find the balance of the certain **Threes** involved that allow them to minimize the victim / perpetrator aspects,

Living In Three

and become their own personal savior. Finding and balancing the **Threes** all around us is the solution to many of our problems, from the most simple to those that change the world.

Look for **Three**. Try and find the different energies of **Three**. Remember, they are that which makes some thing, concept, or energy move in the same direction; that which makes some thing, concept, or energy change direction; or that which makes the thing, concept, or energy stand still. Always be aware that standing still is not natures way and is almost always the wrong thing to do. But in rare cases it's just what needs to be done.

Don't become a victim of your own perpetrations.

Don't become so blind by your faith that you become a perpetrator of harm on others.

But most of all, don't loose yourself in inaction, do nothing, and find yourself on the other side of life saying, "Wow, how could I have been so blind!"

CHAPTER FOUR
COUNTING DOWN: TWO

Two is a perfect number. It is **One** with a partner. It is both sides of everything — and everything does have two sides. It is one of the most important concepts anyone can understand.

All even numbers can be divided by two with a whole number result, as you know. What you might not know is that all whole beings can be divided by two with an even result!

There are divine mysteries of a scared nature concerning **Two** as well. The

Counting Down: Two

union between male and female is a sacred **Two**. If it were not, life could not be created.

A man and a woman take each other in a physical way and two parts of their bodies interact to create life. Two cells of their being combine. Two sets of genes mix. Two individuals create life. This doesn't have to happen with love, as the world knows far to well.

It is also easy to see, because male / female physical representation of **Two** is not limited to humans. Although some animals mate with true love and compassion, there are some who mate purely due to physical reaction to hormonal stimulus. One interesting side bar to this, is the fact that people consider that primates are closer to them emotionally than any other animals. Yet by far, birds choose one mate and stay with that mate for life, raising families and even copulating when there is no possibility of pregnancy to occur.

Another divine mystery of **Two** can also be seen in the great love one individual can have for another. Though it is true one person can love many people in their lifetime, and they do love many people in their life time, each person will have just one great love. Each person has one complete soul mate who they will, if they are lucky, connect with. Some people will live their lives, experiencing love, but never finding this *Love of All Loves*. They will never know they have not experienced it.

Those who love, then meet this great love will know the difference. This love is one that is more than emotional and heart felt. It is a soul love. This soul love is something that can only be experienced with that one other soul who is the other half of your own personal equation of this manifestation of the divine mystery of **Two**.

The other will be the balance of this **Two** in your life. They may or may not be physically compatible to your sexual presence. This means that just because you may be a man, does not mean that this great love will be a woman. In fact, since you are both aspects of a higher unified soul with much of the same likes and attitudes, it is just as likely, if not more so, that you chose the same sex bodies. This isn't to say that you will become sexually active with this person. It is a very common misconception that you must sexually love someone to have

Counting Down: Two

the most deepest of love relationships with them. This is not true. If you are a man, your greatest love, the complement to your soul, could end up being your brother, father or best male friend. If you are a woman, the complement to the **Two** of your soul could be your sister, mother or best girl friend.

To know this person as your closest friend, unwavering companion, and perhaps even your lover, is to know the perfection of this type of **Two**. The greatest loss anyone can have on this Earth is the loss of this person from the living world.

This is because once the twin souls of this **Two** meet, they are forever bonded. So when one passes out of life, the one remaining loses more than someone they love deeply. They are cutting their own twin soul in half, dividing it between the world of the living and what is beyond. So strong is this power of **Two** that in most cases, the one left behind will soon follow the first into the afterlife.

Continuing on our examination of the male / female duality that is a divine mystery of **Two**, there are other forms of the male / female balance. Purely in an energy sense, it is clear to anyone who is a man or woman and who has ever interacted with a person of the opposite sex that men and women are just plain different. The differences can be so different — particularly when the balance of **Two** between a male and female energy force collide — that whole books were written on how to cope with each other.

But despite what the books say, men and women come from the same planet. Moreover, their energy comes from the same perfect duality of **Two**. It is their inability to understand and balance the diametrically charged component of that energy that makes maintaining harmony on the duality problematical.

The energies the female brings to the union are aspects that are often thought of as positive and enriching, such as maternal instincts, creative force, patience, prudence, and the ability to love unconditionally. The energy that the male brings to the union are aspects that are also thought of as desirable, such as reason, strength, action force — that being the energy that brings change — and the ability to love with the deepest of passions.

Counting Down: Two

Aspects of male and female energy that are often thought of as negative, but are in truth not totally undesirable, are — for the male — greed, want, quest for enjoyment over striving to achieve, lust, and ego. For female energy, the list includes, indecision, weakness, fear of facing discord, and envy.

Actually, all people, regardless of their sexual energy, have all these good and not so good attributes. It is the balance of these energies in any given person's personality that indicates if they are of male of female energy. It is usually the case, but not always, that male energy is housed in a male body. Likewise, female energy is housed in a female body. However, there are exceptions.

Another divine mystery of **Two** involves the dual nature of God. The majority of religions western people are exposed to have some concept of God. By and large, that concept is almost universally that of a male God. God is the father. God is the male Creator. And in Christianity, there is also God the son, and God the perceived male spirit called the Holy Ghost.

As if to bring the pendulum full swing back in the other direction, many of the more recently renovated pagan and earth-based religions see an all female Creator — God the Mother, or Mother Goddess.

Regrettably, both extremes are perversions of the balance of the concept of **Two** that is the divine mystery of the nature of God. By removing the female energy from the equation, male deity based belief systems remove the aspects of female energy including the maternal nurturing characteristics that temper the angry God of hellfire and damnation. By removing the creative force and unconditional love of the female from the male archetype of God, man creates a God who is quick to destroy, but slow to create. He is a God that is easy to anger and quick to dole out punishment. He is a God who is unfair in his methods for choosing who he considerers his children and who will be arbitrarily forsaken.

In the most recent incarnations of the pagan religions, the lack of male energy is just as obvious. One thing that is important to remember is that both male and female based religions all began in the same place. That is the place where **Two** was balanced.

Long before the Bible was written, and long before the druids danced in their first circle, the origin of all people's faith was rooted in the dual nature of God. The divine mystery of **Two**, — the two energies of one God — was understood.

What happened that divided people? What made the people of long ago make a conscious decision to remove one whole side of the duality of their God from their belief system?

Archeologists will tell you that there is more than enough evidence to prove that the root faiths of just about every western religion today started as a faith that believed in either a two sexed God or a male and female God who governed over Earth, side by side in harmony.

Human societies were simple, money was not invented yet, and small communities had small needs that were easily met inside their own family units. This natural simplicity fostered and was fostered by a balanced understanding of the concepts of

One: Discovering the True Nature of The Universal Accord

Three by the people. Family units were balanced, communities were balanced, and life was, as a rule, as easy as living in the stone age could be.

This balance continued into their religious belief. They understood that in order to have a productive marriage you needed a man and a woman. They understood that in order for the crops to grow, both seed and soil was necessary. They understood that the energy of the water (male) and the land (female) made life possible. Men and women each had their own duties and place in society.

The male population was functional as hunters, merchants, and workers. The female population was functional as gatherers, mothers, and homemakers. The balance worked.

If you read the last two sentences and find yourself thinking I must be a sexist or male chauvinist or the like, then you have been fooled into the illusion that destroyed the male / female balance and removed the duality from the concept of God and religion. That is, you believe that it is belittling to women to be a gatherer, mother, and homemaker. You have been fooled into thinking the most important jobs that can be done by female energy are worthless. You have bought into the lie that it is more important to make money, succeed in business, and make a name for yourself in the eyes of the world, than to nurture children with values and love, and make a safe, comfortable place where the unity of the family — that all important **Three** that it is — can thrive and grow.

It was just that type of thinking, the thinking that the job women did was not as important as the job that men did, that was used to convince women to give up their power to men, bury their energy, and allow male energy to take over everything — even the world and God. Likewise, men were quick to exploit this attitude and promote the concept that women's work was valueless as a way to control an energy they did not understand.

Women can give birth. This is something that no man can do. This is a power that is strictly female in nature.

Men felt the need to control that too. This is why until modern science came into being, it was commonly taught that a man provided all the material to make a baby in his semen, and a woman was just a human oven. Yet, when a child was born that had any defect, even if that defect was the fact that it was female, it was the mother's fault. Many a Queen lost her life because the Kings semen was rich in female sperm.

By belittling, discrediting or otherwise removing the power of women, men of the time created a world that was harsh, cold and violent. Over time, women were relegated to the status of property, eventually they became liabilities and burdens.

Though you might think that things have changed, and women have equal rights, this is not so. The devolvement of women continues today all over the world. The most extreme examples can be found in the Middle East and East Asian countries where most women are considered barely human and baby girls are often put to death at the moment of their birth. But these are not the only places where women's rights, or more importantly, female energy is being destroyed. It is being destroyed all around you, and you probably never noticed it.

Counting Down: Two

How? You ask. Female energy is still considered negative and undesirable in the "modern" world.

Women who choose the path that enhances their female energies, thus choosing to stay at home and raise their children, are often considered to be lazy, simple minded, and not motivated by the rest of the world. Women who choose their female energies and forgo personal gain to raise their children at home, rather than put them in daycare, are often perceived as shiftless, uneducated and unable to make it in the working world.

Even women who have jobs, but work in careers that are typically considered woman's work, such as nursing, are not given the same respect men in similar jobs are. For example, if you show anyone a man and a woman then ask them to identify who is the doctor and who is the nurse, they are likely to pick the man as the doctor, assuming that the lesser position would be staffed by the woman.

The working woman often feels obligated to put her career before her children. She is deceived into feeling that the only way to maintain her self esteem is to "make good in a man's world," rather than to mold the next generation. She is tricked into giving up her female power, in some cases to even despise her female energy.

This is not to say that women don't have a right or need to have a job or career. Indeed, it is their right if they wish it. The caution here is that women need to realize that they have been brainwashed by time and the ages into believing that they have no value to humanity if they don't have a career, make money, and make a name for themselves in a male dominated way. If they can do all that and keep their dual nature in balance, that is a wonderful thing. But more often than not, they do not.

There is nothing wrong with women being women. Indeed, if men could be men and be satisfied with that, and not long to be the masters of female energy as well as their own male energy, there would be no problem. When the strong motivation and ambition for power that comes with male energy, and the reluctance to make strife or engage in disagreements that marks the female energy come together, it is very easy for the balance to go out of proportion as the

Counting Down: Two

male energy naturally wants to possess and control, and the female energy is reluctant to fight back, choosing not to risk the peace.

This is why when men used their energy to remove the female energy from the equation of the duality of God, it was allowed. Well, almost. Holdouts to the forsaking of the female embodiment of God formed their own religions, often choosing to drop the male aspect, if only to counter a growing male energy religious movement.

Nevertheless, the duality of male and female energy must be in balance. Unlike the diversity of **Three**, there is only one position that is acceptable in **Two**.

Another divine mystery of **Two** involves the concepts of opposites. Fast or slow, up or down, in or out, stop or go, these are all basic examples of this seemingly simple divine mystery. Everything that is has something opposite to it. Every action has an opposite action. Every front has a back, and everything that goes up, must come down. Straightforward enough, or is it?

If everything has something opposite to it that completes the **Two** involved with it, then that means more than just the opposite of light is dark. It also means that for every light there is a dark. For every front there is a back, for every happiness there is a sorrow, for every good there is an evil. It is unavoidable.

This does not mean that every time you have a happy moment in your life you will be sad in return and to the same degree. But it does mean than for happiness to have any meaning in your life, you will experience sadness to some degree. The degree of sadness a person is forced to endure will cause them to be more aware and appreciative of happiness when they experience it. A person who knows how deep despair can be is more likely to feel the profound nature of joy.

You have heard the saying, "you never know what you have until it is gone." The concept is similar. You cannot know the ultimate of happiness if you have no concept of what loneliness and despair feels like. More exactly, how can you know what happiness truly is if you have never felt its absence? You cannot truly understand it. It would be akin to trying to understand what it is like to experience sitting in a dark room if you have spent your entire life inside a brightly lit room. You could, of course, comprehend what darkness means and your intellectual self would try to envision what it must be like. Still, you can never really know until you experience the real thing.

Likewise, how can any person be good if there is no wickedness to give the concept of good a positive value? Of course, you could say that it is a person's actions that make them good as opposed to bad. But if there is no other behavior to compare it to, how could you make that determination? If everyone was always pure hearted and wholesome, then working to have a pure heart and remain decent would have much less importance than it does in this world of sin and strife.

Another divine mystery of **Two** is that of giver and taker. Like most divine mysteries, it sounds a lot more straight forward than it often is. This divine mystery comes with a responsibility that many people do not honor or take serious. If more people did, the world around you would be a much better place.

In each person's life there will be times when they are takers and givers. Some of the most obvious examples of period in your life when you are a taker most of the time is during your infancy and childhood. Infants and children are naturally takers. They have many needs and are, even after infancy, almost entirely unable to care for themselves. They cannot and are not expected to return the energy given by way of effort and work which is expended on them by the givers who complete this **Two** in their lives. They are helpless during this period of their life and this is understood by their parents and older family members.

If the balance of this all important **Two** is to be maintained correctly, in time, when the children grow and become adults, they will return the energy and effort taking care of not only the next generation of children, but also their aging elders who, in time, will not be able to care for themselves. Far to often, the second part of this **Two** is ignored by modern society, causing an imbalance that is harmful to the important **Three** of the family unit.

There are other divine mysteries of **Two**. I am sure you will find them if you

Counting Down: Two

look around you, thinking of the concept of **Two**. The common characteristic of all examples of **Two** is that they will be equal and opposite in order to be in correct balance. Keep this in mind in order to balance any divine mystery of **Two**.

CHAPTER FIVE
LIVING IN TWO

Living in **Two**, in theory is simple. To live in **Two**, you have to uncover the dual elements that must be in balance, then put them in balance. Simple in theory, but very difficult to live.

One of the first **Two** you probably have to face is that of the giver and taker. It's a good example to start with because it protrudes into the physical world in many ways. Of course, there are non-physical aspects of this **Two**, such as giving and taking emotional energies. But for now, let's look at some of the more physical aspects of this **Two**.

It is not good enough when speaking of the balance of this divine mystery of **Two** to simply say, "Today, I'm a taker. Maybe next week I'll give." You have to try and be aware when you are taking so that you can remember to give in return. If this sounds like some kind of cosmic bank loan, you could be over simplifying the concept and setting yourself up to fall into an imbalance.

Obviously, if you go to a bank and borrow money, you will have to give it back in time, and with interest. This seems to be the same concept as what I said about takers needing to keep track of their taking in order to give enough to keep the balance. But in truth, it is not a matter of accounting limits as it is a matter of giving everything.

It has been said and it is good to remember a simple rule, "When you need, you should be allowed to take without shame and embarrassment. When you have no need, you should give without selfishness or limitation." Then this divine mystery of **Two** will work.

We all should watch how much we take and try to be conscious to give back in order to keep our mind clear that taking is not a way of life, and that taking when you really don't need it is wrong. Far too often, people who are in the taking mode learn to make a living from it. They take physically, financially, emotionally, even spiritually. They take and take and take, never giving back, sometimes feeling cheated, unfairly put upon, and possibly even robbed if they are ever in a position where giving is required from them.

Oddly enough, there are people who are just as poorly balanced as givers. They give and give and give, never allowing people to do for themselves. By allowing others to become dependent on their giving, they gain control over the takers. Often because of deep emotional need — usually caused by an imbalance of one or more **Threes** in their life — they find their own self-esteem and personal power in the illusion they present to others that they are selfless, and all sacrificing.

These super-takers and super-givers feed each other's imbalance. If they were a microcosm onto themselves there would be no problem. If that were the case, then we could say they were just another form of the giver / taker **Two** divine mystery that is playing out in two separate populations of people. Unfortunately, this is not the case. People who are super-takers and super-givers have motives that are not helpful to their spiritual growth. The super-taker suffers from selfishness and lack of motivation. The super-giver suffers from an abnormally driven ego, fueled by an underlying need to control others.

It doesn't matter if a person is a super-giver or a super-taker, their balance of **Two** is way off kilter, not to mention several **Threes** including the divine mystery of Victim, Savior, Perpetrator.

A healthy balance of the giver / taker divine mystery of **Two** is easy to see in the relationship of a mother and infant. The good mother gives to the infant without being told she must. She loves the child unconditionally, regardless of the child's beauty or physical perfection. A mother is willing to give to her child to the extent of giving her own life. The child takes without thinking about it. In fact, the child doesn't even realize it is taking. The fact that a child doesn't know it is taking, gives it the freedom to take without concern or limit. The mother gives because it is her obligation

One: Discovering the True Nature of The Universal Accord

and because of her love. The child takes because it is the child's nature. It is a bit more tricky when the giver and taker are both of an age to understand that they are giving and taking.

If you know you are taking, you have a few responsibilities. The most obvious is that you must remember to find a way to return the gesture. This doesn't mean that if your friend buys you lunch on Monday, you have to buy him lunch next Monday; even though this is probably required by proper etiquette, and is a nice thing to do. What I mean by saying you have to return the gesture can be seen in the example of a family who has fallen on hard times. They have trouble making ends meet and they are strapped for cash to buy their groceries. Due to these circumstances, they find themselves at a Salvation Army soup kitchen. For several weeks they have no choice but to go to the soup kitchen to feed their family. Weeks later, the head of the household gets a new job and the family starts to get back on their feet. Months later, they are finally starting to catch up with their back due bills. In a year or two, the family is once again doing well and they are not worried about their next meal or afraid they will loose their home. They still don't have the money to buy that new in-ground pool, but they are not suffering anymore. The balance of this divine mystery of **Two** requires them, now that they are no longer in need, to make the effort to help others.

This does not mean that they need to go into the hole, spending all their money on feeding the poor. But it does require every member of the family in their own way, to their own abilities, to help others who are now less fortunate than they are. This could be as simple as occasionally putting a few cans of corn into the soup kitchen collection bin when they buy groceries, or as involved as volunteering at a shelter for the homeless. Both efforts are just as valid. The physical effort put into giving is not as important as the intent behind the giving. To give your all is not always to give in a showy or complicated way.

Another obligation you have when you are in the position of taking is to take with pride. Never allow anyone to take your personal power away from you by making you feel like you are less worthy of life because you are in a position where you have to take. If you do this, you run the risk

One: Discovering the True Nature of The Universal Accord

that you are going to allow another person to control you. You also risk the chance that you will loose your self-esteem to the extent that you will be fooled into becoming a habitual taker.

When you are in the position of being a taker, it is your duty to take with a sense of self-respect and not to take what you do not need. Also, it is good to remember that you do not have to take just because someone is giving something to you. You always have the right to say, "No, thank you."

On the other side of this **Two**, there are some things you should know about being a giver. As with the role of the taker, there are pitfalls to avoid when being a giver.

The first and most dangerous pitfall to being a giver is that of thinking because you can give and another must take, that you are better than they are. You are not. Similarly, just because someone has to take from you doesn't mean they are inferior to you. If you start thinking this way, it will not be long before your ego gets out of control and you begin to believe that you are giving to help others, but you are truly giving to make yourself feel superior. In that event, your own self-respect and self-esteem will be lost, and soon the only way you will be able to feel a sense of self respect and esteem is by belittling those around you. The terrible downward spiral caused by this **Two** imbalance is very hard to break out of.

Some of the symptoms that you could be already riding this spiral down include the feeling that what you don't want anymore is "good enough" for those who are in need. Of course, that coat you wore only once and is in great shape might be a godsend to a homeless person who is totally without a way to keep warm. If you give with that in mind, it has been given in the correct frame of mind. But when you dig out a few cans of twenty-year-old lima beans from the dusty shelf in your basement for the food drive, thinking with a flavor of disdain; "They are good enough for the poor," or "Beggars can't be choosers," you are clearly on the this destructive spiral. It is clear that food that is not good enough for you is — in your mind — good enough for "them". You have put yourself over others. Your attempt at charity and giving is not only useless to your own soul and personal growth, but in all likelihood to the recipient of your "gift".

One: Discovering the True Nature of The Universal Accord

Every day the poor across many nations throw away dusty twenty-year-old cans of lima beans and other such things they won't eat either.

Before you give, ask yourself, "Is this something I would be ashamed to hand to the person if I had to give it to him face to face?" If so, don't give it. Also, it is good to ask yourself if you are giving because you feel it is the right thing to do, or because you expect people to take notice of how wonderful you are because you give such gifts.

You may be one of the many people who have never been in the position to take anything given from the charity of others, and you may be wondering how this applies to you. In fact, this applies all the more. That you have never needed to be on the taking end of this equation in a physical sense shows that you have been given such good fortune by God. You have taken from God without even knowing it. Thus, in return, you should give in the spirit of God to those who have not been given as much of a physical nature as you have.

Living in Two

The balance of this giver / taker cycle can also be seen in the spiritual side of our lives as well. How often we cycle through the unending drama created by this all important **Two** and how intense or painful it can be, depends on how well we handle ourselves and how well we understand the mechanics of the **Two** itself.

Emotionally, we give all the time. We give of our emotions in different degrees with every conversation and interaction we have with others. They give of their own emotions in return. Sometimes it is obvious, such as when you share a personal moment with a friend or lover. Other times it is less apparent, such as when you talk to a telemarketer over the phone. Nevertheless, in both situations you are giving and taking emotional energy.

You should try to maintain a balance between the type of energy you give and the type you take. If you do not maintain the balance of this manifestation of **Two**, your emotional state will begin to suffer. If proportions get too far out of whack you will find yourself becoming bitter, angry, unhappy, depressed, or any combination of these terrible states of being.

Worst yet, you will be so emotionally charged with these nasty attributes that you will have no choice but to project them onto others. More often than not, those others will be people who are open and receptive to you, such as your family and friends. The saying, "You always hurt the ones you love," is very true, if only because they care about you enough to be hurt by your words, attitudes and moods.

How often in your life have you found this happening? How many times have you had a bad day at work, your car broke down, an unexpected bill came in that you didn't have money for, or you woke up sick on a day when you really had to get something important done? As you deal with the unpleasant situation, all your years of working on your higher self start to fall apart, and sooner or later you find yourself tired, upset, and frustrated with the situation. Eventually, someone in your life crosses your path and does something small that normally would not infuriate your. Then, for no reason of their making, all the emotional turmoil in you bubbles up like a volcano and erupts out of you in waves of anger and frustration.

Living in Two

I would hope you are able to control the frustration and cope — holding back, not spreading your negative emotional state to the other. But we must admit, there are times when we do not hold back, and our loved one gets hit with a tidal wave of negative emotion.

Luckily, negative emotions tend to pass quickly if we just let them. This is probably the only thing that really saves us all from being terrible miserable people all the time, because the world is so bombarded with terrible, negative images, and each person is surrounded by matter and items that invoke a negative emotional response in people who experience them.

Whether a thing or event is specifically designed to bring into play negative emotions or if it's simply an unplanned side effect doesn't matter. The results are the same. People who are exposed will experience a rise in the negative side of this **Two**.

Of course, there are thing, events and images in this world that will invoke a positive and happy emotional state just as strongly. But these things don't seem to be as obvious on a day to day basis. It is not because there are fewer of them or that they are harder to find. It is just that — oddly enough — people are drawn to the things that cause negative emotions. As any newsperson will tell you, good news doesn't sell papers or bring up television ratings. Why? Because people don't care about things when they are going good, only when they are going bad. This makes sense when you think that people believe that news is something they "need" to know in order to be prepared and informed. You really don't need to know what is going right with the world in order to be prepared. You need to know what could cause your life to be in danger.

But what about movies, television shows and other forms of entertainment? Why are they so negative this days? Why aren't most people happy watching shows like "Leave It To Beaver" or "The Brady Bunch" where all the problems of life are small, people are generally always happy, no one is ever seriously hurt or ill, and everything that could go wrong is neatly solved in 30 minutes or less? Why do people rush to watch reality TV shows, live

Living in Two

emergency room action, and police in the act of taking down real live criminals? Why do so many people relish the violence of movies where they are assailed with visions of other human beings being shot, dismembered or otherwise killed in the most unspeakable ways?

The answer can be found in basic human chemistry. Because people have been raised for the last few generations, from an early age, to believe that the adrenalin rush produced by the natural *fight, flee or die* response their body produces when it is exposed to negative types of stimulus is a pleasant thing, they have come to enjoy the feeling. This adrenalin rush is based on a natural, animal response that is pre-programmed into the survival skills of the physical body. That programming is triggered by the body's perceived fear that it is in a situation where it has to either fight, run away, or be killed. This fear is produced inside the brain by the information coming through the senses. In the case of a blood filled movie, the eyes see carnage and the ears hear horror and screaming of the dying. In the case of a reality television show, the eyes see people pushed to the limit of stress as they deal with life or death situations, and the ears hear strained, panicked voices. Even with something as simple as an amusement park ride, the forces on the outside of the body tell the brain it is in a life or death situation.

Even though the intellect of the person watching the movie or sitting on the roller coaster know that they are in no real danger, the primal force in their body that controls the fight, flee or die reaction does not know this. It fears the worse and in an effort to give the body the boost it needs to try and survive the perceived threat, it pumps up the juices. These juices make the person involved in the stimulus feel a rush of emotional energy, excitement, and even a feeling of "wow, I survived it!" The energy of these emotional states is strong. In the true sense. it is nature's way of rewarding the body for surviving.

Unfortunately, like any system in the body, the system that controls the fight, flee or die function adapts over time. Sooner or later, the body is going to figure out that riding a carousel is not life threatening, and the person will need to ride something faster to invoke the same reaction. Eventually, they will get use to that as well. Given enough time, they will find that they must go on the fastest, highest roller coaster to even hope to get the same level of thrill they once got from the merry-go-round.

The excitement, fear, and sense of suspense that past generations of children got when they watched Beaver Cleaver try to hide a scratch on the family car from his parents, is something that the current generation finds ridiculous. Is it really because the current generation is more sophisticated as some would have you believe? No. It is because over time and generations, we teach our children based on our limits of fear. Just as over time bodies become accustomed to things that provoked a fear response at one time, mankind is learning, over generations, to be less and less effected by those things around them that create negative situations and fear response.

What does all this have to do with **Two**? It has a lot to do with it. Since it is clear, based on the physical need to develop, as time goes on, more and more fear invoking stimulus in the media and entertainment world, it is certain that the amount of negative influences around you will only increase if you continue to expose yourself to these stimuli.

This is not to say that you must isolate yourself from all this stuff in order to stay balanced. In fact, I believe it would be hard for all but the very few of you who have financial independence and complete spiritual freedom to isolate yourself from all such images and stimuli. Also, you may be one of the individuals who takes joy in the occasional roller coaster ride, and it really is not necessary to deny yourself that simple pleasure. If you find excitement in a good action movie full of explosions and shootings, so long as you can isolate the reality from the fiction and keep the balance of this important aspect of **Two** in perspective, even these visions of negative origin will not hurt you in the long run.

The danger comes into play when you allow yourself to be bombarded by these negative natured forms of entertainment and information without taking time to expose yourself to the other side of the balance. For every negative you are exposed to you must take time to experience a positive. When you get off that roller coaster, you may want to take a few moments to sit and look at the

Living in Two

beauty of a flower or the divine simplicity of the blue sky above your head.

You must be constantly aware that it is in human nature to gravitate to the excitement of the negative, rather than to the sublime nature of the positive. In order to keep this important aspect of **Two** in balance you make the effort to find the inspirational, bathe your eyes in the beauty of the natural and listen to the sound of harmony in whatever form you choose.

You will find in time, as you expose yourself more and more to the awe-inspiring aspects of the world that inspire joy and serenity in your body along with the long lasting endorphins these emotions will release into your system, you will have less and less need for the short adrenaline rush produced by the negative.

You might be surprised to know that you can be out of balance in this good direction as well. If you are, you are likely not to see danger that is standing right in front of you and may find yourself getting hurt a lot by others — maybe to the extent of loosing your life because you just could not perceive the danger before you, simply because your balance was so far to this side that you no longer had a functioning fight, flee or die instinct.

So, though it is always better to err on the positive side if you cannot maintain a balance, never let your balance go so far off that you become a victim of yourself or others.

One last aspect of **Two** that is often confusing to put into life's action is that of good and evil. This divine aspect of **Two** is usually misunderstood by most people.

It is obvious that good and evil are opposites. It might not be as obvious that they are also complementary. Just like you cannot give if there is no one to receive, you cannot be good if there is no evil to help define the limits of what good is.

In the truest form, there is no middle ground between good and evil. A thing, event, or energy that can be classified as either good or evil is always either one or the other. There is no neutral in-between good or evil. If something that could be good or evil is not good or evil it is not the balance between good and evil. Rather, it is the nullification of good and evil. Though it might seem like a balance, a nullification — in this sense — is not a **Two** or even a **Three**, but a **One**.

CHAPTER SIX
COUNTING DOWN: ONE

Before we talk about exactly what **One** is, it may do some good to discuss what **One** is not. Of course, **One** is not **Two** or **Three**. But **One** is also not singular. When we speak about **One** try not to think of **One** in terms of being "the one and only" or "one and apart from all". **One** —in the framework of the singular point of view — may truly be the loneliness number. In the true aspects of **One**, it is anything but lonely.

One is not singluar in the sense that singular means alone. **One** is never alone. Yet, there is nothing like **One** or even with

Counting Down: One

One. **One** is all things, so it is one thing and many things at the same time.

One — in this sense — is not the first thing in a list. More accurately, it is not just the first thing in the list. It is the second, third, fourth, and more. It is everything in the list. **One** is not a solitary object or concept in the way you might conceive of when you think of one object or idea standing by itself in an endless sea of nothingness.

Unfortunately, it can be very difficult for us not to picture **One** as being solitary and isolated. Worse yet, it is hard not to think of **One** as standing by itself on a pedestal, above the reach of everyday people.

Maybe when you, like many others, think of concepts that are clearly **One**, you may envision yourself in a place of ultimate privacy, perhaps sitting by a gently flowing brook or floating on a peaceful, downy cloud, communing with the Universal Order. It could be that when you imagine what it must be like to connect to **One**, you may see in your mind's eye that it is like being embraced by the arms of God, or flying to the heavens on newly discovered wings of an angel.

One always seems like a very unique and personal experience we make as individuals to connect with our own individual and unique concept of God. But, **One** is more than this.

You know how many are in the number one. You know how much one is in the physical world. One is a single unit. But in the greater picture of what is going on in the universe, **One** is more than a single thing. **One** is the Universal Accord of many things. Actually, it is the Universal Accord of All things.

What is a Universal Accord, you ask? Who make it up? How do you become part of it? The answers are right before you, and inside you. The Universal Accord, is simply an agreed state of being that happens when **One** occurs. We are all an equal part of it. It does not matter if you are a human, an angel or an ant, we are all equal parts of the same Universal Accord. You have to do nothing to become part of it. You are already part of it. You only have to understand what it is, and claim your place in it's existence to be aware you are part of it.

"What," I imagine you may say, "how can an ant be an equal to a human in the Universal Accord?"

In return I ask you, "How can a human be an equal to an angel in the Universal Accord?"

To the Universal Accord, each and every part of it is an equal part of it. It does not matter what level of consciousness the human mind can conceive the animal, insect, or heavenly being having. Simply because humankind cannot wrap their minds around the concept that an ant could have an understanding of the meaning of its own life does not diminish the ant in the eyes of the Universal Accord.

Humankind and the Universal Accord have different standards. This is probably a good thing, because it is likely if humans were truly judged by the standards they hold other species to, they would find out the hard way how far down the totem pole they are — if only because the standards used to judge them would be based on superficial things like body type, size, and physical abilities. Using these criteria, human beings would be considered quite backwards and insect-like to many races that are more evolutionarily and technologically advanced.

All things that exist and have energy, no matter what form that existence and energy takes, are equal partners in the Universal Accord. Energy can be active, such as in the souls of living things, or it can be dormant, as in many man-made objects. Regardless if the energy is dormant or active, it is still important to the agreement made in order for the Universe to exist. The Universal Accord is the energies that make up that agreement.

Why was an agreement needed? Simple, there had to be a plan to the Universe. There had to be an order. Everything had to make sense, work together, and complement everything else. Energy could not take on random forms and functions with no consideration for the form and functions taken on by other energies. If it did, it would be unproductive to the purpose of the whole. So, when Creation decided to happen, it first made a plan. It produced the Universal Accord — the blueprint of the universe and all that is.

Everything that ever existed, everything that exists now, and everything that will ever exist, in any space, time or dimension that is part of God's creation is part of the Universal Accord. It is a piece of the plan — a line on the blueprint.

An energy might be as small as a tiny nail in the wood of the hull of a great ship, or it might be as big as the anchor, but it is necessary to the whole. As you know, take all the tiny nails out of the ships hull and it will fall apart and sink. Remove one or two nails and you might not think you are doing much harm, but even though it is not obvious and evident, you have comprised the design. Eventually, if you do not realize what you have done and continue to remove nails, the whole ship will fall apart, possibly without warning.

I only mention this because people are quick to feel confident that because they removed one or two or a hundred nails and the ship still floats, they can pull out more. Of course, I am not talking about a boat in this case. I am talking about the Earth, to which the analogy of a boat is curiously appropriate. After all, it is the vehicle people use to voyage around the sun; and people are constantly removing the nails that hold her together in the form of mining, pollution, overpopulation and destruction of natural resources.

If the concept of **One** were understood and respected, if even just a little bit, by all people of the Earth, the nail pulling would slow greatly, possibly even stop all together.

There are divine mysteries of **One**, just as there are divine mysteries of **Two** and **Three**. The divine mysteries of **One** are often a bit harder to see in our lives. This is not because there are so few of them, or because they are so complex, but rather, because they are very simple and are easily put aside as unimportant.

Some of the most common divine mysteries of **One** can be found in our birth and death. The crossing over into and out of human life are one-time events. Though some religions use the term "born again", you are truly only born into this life one time. You will only pass out of this life one time. No more, no less.

Yes, it is true that some people have had near death experiences and have claimed to returned from the dead. Though it should be understood that these fortunate individuals have not actually returned from the dead, but rather from the near dead. They did not make the complete journey into the spirit world. Had they crossed completely over, the connection between their souls and their bodies would have been broken. Much like the umbilical cord between the infant and the placenta is cut upon birth. When this cord is broken, the body can no longer support a soul and the body will die. This is unavoidable. The cord cannot be reconnected. If this cord is not cut, the person is not truly dead in the most final of ways.

This is not to say that their experience isn't real. It is. You can see the other side from these states. And so long as the cord is not broken, you can return to this side, provided your body is capable of sustaining life.

People who have seen the other side have a powerful advantage. They know beyond a doubt that there is life beyond the physical. They know beyond the slightest hesitation or that nagging voice of "reason" that there is more. This is something most people struggle with at one time or another in their life. That is not to say that they don't believe in a life after death, but believing in something is not always as strong and stable a force as seeing it first hand.

Every human being on this planet has experienced birth. Birth happened to us each in our turn. It was the doorway from which we entered physical life. We were surrounded by the energy of others. Our mother was there for sure. Our father, if we were lucky. Maybe a doctor and some nurses greeted us upon our arrival. Still, even for those who are one of a set of twins, each of us is born alone. Each of us takes our first breath that activates that cord that connects our particular soul permanently to our particular body by ourselves. We cannot have anyone help us. We just do it, without even knowing how. Even if a doctor or nurse helps us draw our first breath, that fastening of our soul to the body is done entirely by ourselves and ourselves alone. This is a divine **One**.

Counting Down: One

When we die, we pass out of this world just as alone as we passed into it. Even if you were to die simultaneously with a hundred other people, even if your deaths occurred at the exact same moment in time, you would not die together. The act of release would happen to each individual individually.

Another divine mystery of **One** can be found in our growing to a spiritual goal. Our journey to that goal is always our own. Though we may share our journey with others, we are truly the only ones we can help. Even if you think all your endless words are going to help people find their path, you cannot really lead anyone. Even this book, and my words in it, are not going to bring you closer to your spiritual goal. It is not the words or the information in books, it is what YOU do with those words and information that bring you down your path. When you get to the end of your journey, only you will know. No one can tell you that you have succeeded. No one can tell you that you have arrived.

Paradoxically, you cannot make your spiritual journey alone. I know it sounds like I am contradicting everything I just said, but I am not. To understand why, you must understand another divine mystery of **One**.

Probably the most important mystery of **One** that you will need to know in order to understand the concept of **One** as a whole is the fact that everything that is **One** is rooted in a paradox. I know this sounds rather strange. That is probably because people are not use to having to deal with paradoxes. Rather, they try to resolve them to be one way or another.

Some of the paradoxes created by **One** almost seem like riddles created to confuse those who ponder **One**. Others seem to lack the depth that most of them have. For example, a paradox that is in play in the divine mystery of **One** that concerns birth and death is that by being born, you are creating your own death.

Since this time in an earth bound body is a temporary condition for the energy of your soul, then by the very fact that you have taken on this temporary condition through birth, you have also condemned yourself to death. Thus, to be born is to die. That birth is the reason for death is a rather shallow paradox, and probably does not cause you to ponder very long on the concept. It is a paradox that, although a bit ironic, is not essentially hard to understand.

A paradox that comes into play with the idea of the spiritual path is a bit more complex and bears a longer look at. In short, the journey to a spiritual goal is an individualized matter that is unique to the person experiencing it. No one can really lead you on this journey. No one can tell you where to go with any certainty that it is the correct way for you. The paradox comes into play when you realize that without the contact and interactions with others, you will never find all the things you need to make your way on this journey. Without others to reveal information to you, give you suggestions, and share their journey with you, you would not be able to get where you are going.

If your journey was one you could do without any assistance, you would not be seeking knowledge and assistance. Yet, all the knowledge poured upon you and all the assistance you are given will not bring you one step closer to your goal — a paradox.

Another divine mystery of **One** concerns the Universal Force itself. God is all things. It is collectively agreed that

One: Discovering the True Nature of The Universal Accord

Creation, God, the Universal Intelligence, whatever name you want to use, is all things. God is the ultimate, the alpha and omega. God is eternal. God has always been, and will always be. There is no end or limits to that which is God.

This said, it is also collectively agreed that God created everything. That it was God — or the creative intelligence of the almighty — that gave form to the universe. In other words, God planned, wrote and executed the Universal Accord.

Paradoxical indeed that God, who is all things, also created all things. Yet, though it is hard for us to understand how, we accept this divine mystery of **One** without question.

We rationalize the belief in a celestial intelligence working behind the scenes, planning and creating the universe around us in many ways. We have all grown up, learning about science and the logical, physical rules humankind uses to define the world. Yet when we look at the intricate design of a honeysuckle flower's pedals, we are amazed by how they are perfectly formed to hold the nectar needed by the humming bird who hovers by it feeding. We are amazed about how the beak seems to be created to fit the very flower in front of the bird. It is then, as we watch in wonder, we realize that despite the fact that science directs us to believe in natural selection and the evolution of species, we know in our hearts that there is an order to Creation. The blueprint of all that is, hovers before us in the form of this small feeding bird and the bright and fragrant blossom it feeds from.

We understand that there is a force of creation that made all things, yet we fail to ponder — perhaps because we simply cannot comprehend — that the Creation and the Creator are not just inseparable but are, in fact, identical. They are the same. They are **One**.

Another divine mystery of **One** is all around you. In fact, it is you. You are a divine mystery of **One**. You are a totally unique individual. Even if you have an identical twin, your twin and you may be physically identical, but the two of you are still different and distinct people.

Moreover, you have a soul. That soul, like every other soul in the universe, is eternal. It is complex and complete. Complete in eternal terms means that your soul has everything in it — everything.

The paradox is that everyone else who has a soul has the same complete nature to their souls as well. Thus, if their souls are everything, and your soul is everything, your soul is actually identical to theirs. Though you are totally unique, you are also exactly the same as every other soul in creation.

One is so overflowing with paradoxes it is difficult to pin down exactly what **One** is without becoming confused by the paradoxes that define the concept you are exploring.

This becomes a problem for many people because it is natural for you to want to resolve a paradox. Often, it is in the nature of people to disregard paradoxes as lies. They choose to believe that if a thing is paradoxical in nature it is not because it is truly opposite things at one time, but rather that one of those directions must be wrong. Disregarding either or both sides of a paradox takes the **One** out of the situation and removes the wonder, mystery, and power from it.

Counting Down: One

Paradoxes connected with **One** should be explored. There is much to learn from them. In time, you may even find peace with the conflicts they appear to be. But do not be quick to disregard them or believe you have found a resolution to them. If the thing you are examining is truly a mystery of **One**, and you have removed the paradox, you are likely making a mistake in your reasoning, or what you believed was a **One** was actually a **Two**, **Three** or something else.

CHAPTER SEVEN
LIVING IN ONE

Considering the paradoxical nature of **One**, you might assume it a very difficult thing to live in **One**. It would be very confusing if everything you did in your life were a paradox. If every action you took had to do two seemingly opposing things at the same time.

It is a good thing that this is not the way it is. To live in **One** does not mean you have to live constantly in a state of confusion. More to the opposite. To live in **One** is to accept the apparently inconsistency of **One** with faith and to conduct your life with the confidence that both aspects of any **One** are true at the same time.

Returning our attention to some of the Divine Mysteries of **One**, we can try and apply them to our lives so we may live in **One**. Sometimes divine mysteries of **One** do not really require much of us. We simply except them, perhaps not even wanting to understand them. The divine mystery that we are born and therefore will die is a mystery of **One** most of us would rather not linger on. But there is something to learn from it.

This particular mystery of **One** teaches us many things. It teaches us that there is a beginning and an end to our time here on Earth. Although we can dream of physical immortality, we know it can never be. Even with the ultimate of scientific achievements to their credit, immortality is still the stuff of science fiction, not science fact. I am certain — regardless of how much time, effort, and research is put into it — physical immortality is destined to remain in the realm of science fiction forever.

Why am I so certain? I am so certain because the birth / death paradox is a divine mystery of **One**. Because of this, birth and death are inseparable. The only way not to physically die is not to be born into the physical world at all. That is the only way.

This fact can help us in many ways. That is, if we choose to explore it. For example, by realizing that their lives are not unending here on Earth, people have had to develop a culturally understanding of what happens after Earth-life has ended. By offering people as a whole, and separate people as individuals, the opportunity to ponder what will happen to them after they have left human life, this divine mystery of **One** affords people the incentive to explore their personal relationship with the Almighty. By knowing that someday each of us will have to face our Valhalla, each of us is forced to think about our connection to what is beyond this human life. We are forced to ponder our place in the Universal Accord.

As a result of this understanding, people have, over time, discovered and implemented a rule of ethics and behavior. By following these rules the individual can become worthy of attaining this afterlife based heaven. Even if the rules and protocol

Living in One

created by a people's culture miss the mark and do not apply to the overall idea of what is accepted behavior in the greater Accord, the simple act of producing these laws and living by them presents a framework of decency and order to the culture that devised it. The understanding created as a consequence of this divine mystery of **One** proves to be of assistance to the people who explore it.

When you think about it, with few exceptions, the religions of every culture across the face of the world are based on this divine mystery of **One**. Think about what drives most religions. The idea that God is out there, and that someday — in some cases if the follower is deserving enough — he or she will die and return to their God. Or, perhaps, he or she will die and return to Earth in a different form. There are many other ideas, as well. No matter what the eventual destination of the disciple of the faith, the one central united theme is that death will be the doorway to that destination.

One message that should be gleaned clearly from this divine mystery of **One**, but is most often brushed over with a broad quick stroke and forgotten, is that of the reason for birth. Birth was given to each of us in order to bring us into this life, so we can live this life for each day. This living each day for itself is something people do far too little of.

It could be, because from an early age, most people are indoctrinated into believing that their reason for life is to get it over with and get to death so they can go onto their heavenly reward.

It is unfortunate that this is the theme of most major religious movements. The dogma of most religions in taught in such a way that followers are encouraged — even pressured — into believing that the point of life is to do the best you can, enduring life with as few sins as possible, so that someday you can gain some kind of recompense for your suffering.

This thinking has caused plenty of people to feel guilt and shame for having a good time in their lives. Even today, there are countless God fearing people who believe that the true path to heaven is by way of suffering, poverty, pain, and self mutilation. Even the very phrase, "God fearing people" — meaning those good people who do what God wants them to do — is evidence to the fact that for time and memorial people have believed that you must live in fear and suffering of a vengeful God in order to deserve more when you die.

Again, the concept of the purpose of birth is removed from the **One** and the focus is shifted to death and fear of what comes after. Thus, the divine mystery is invalid and the concept is erroneous and therefore no longer in harmony with the Universal Accord, which caused it to be in the first place.

Explore this yourself and you will see that you have probably learned quite a bit due to the simple fact that you know your physical life will someday end. Consider how much of what you know is based on fear of what could happen to you after your death.

Consider this; are you afraid of what could have happened to you before you were born?

So then, to live in harmony with this divine mystery of **One**, each of us must take the time to understand not only that death has a purpose, but that birth and life have one, too. We each have to learn to live for every day — for each moment.

I know you have heard the idea before. Living for the moment is nothing new. But have you truly ever thought about what it means to live for the moment? Few people have.

When you live for the moment, you think about now. You do not worry about two seconds ago. You do not think about two seconds from now. You think about what you are doing, how you are feeling and what you are sensing at this very second in time and only this very second in time.

Do it. Pause for a second of time and truly experience everything around you right now. Do not think about a split second ago. Do not think about the next second. Think about right now. Feel what you are feeling right now.

Did you do it?

Experiencing one second of time is not really that impacting in a person's life. Yet, consider what happens when those seconds start to add up to minutes, then

Living in One

hours, then days, months, years, and decades. The fact that you focused on each one of those seconds of your life will make a difference. You will be living life, not just existing in a physical form for a period of time.

Because of the divine nature of **One** concerning birth and death, birth would have no meaning if life went on forever without death. To be born would be nothing special, because the start of another life would have little importance to anyone — that is, if it happened at all. People would not need children or heirs and a new generation would be a useless thing.

Equally the same, without acknowledging the importance of birth, choosing to focus instead on the eventuality of death, the power of life is taken away from each day we live.

In order to focus on life, we have to understand that there is a divine mystery of **One** relating to life as well. That mystery is that life is for living it and experiencing it physically, and that is all. Yet at the same time, life is our only opportunity based in the

One: Discovering the True Nature of The Universal Accord

physical plane to grow and become more as a spiritual being.

Strange, isn't it? Each living being's only reason for life is to experience what it is to be here, on planet Earth, living each moment, hour, day, year, decade, and lifetime. Nothing more is expected. Nothing more is demanded. Nothing more is even requested. Nevertheless, physical life is each person's only opportunity to discover some very important things that will assist in growth as a spiritual being. Therefore, if each of us do not take that opportunity and make the effort in order to grow, we are not doing the part we agreed to in the Universal Accord. We are shirking our responsibility in the divine blueprint of Creation.

Again, it is a paradox. We are not required or expected to do anything but experience our life here. Yet, if we do nothing more than that, we risk letting the ball drop with respect to our part of the bargain with the Universal Accord.

Moreover, it could be that the only effort the Universal Accord requires of us is to do nothing more than experience life. If this is so, then additional efforts could be for no good purpose. Nevertheless, the paradoxical quality of **One**, by its very nature, obliges us to understand that we must experience the fullness of life as our only focus to the purpose of life, and at the same time requires us to take what we learn and apply it to our own perpetual spiritual growth. This in turn assists the development of the agenda of the Universal Accord.

This means we are required to do both if we want to live in **One**. We are required to both live only for the moment, only for life itself; and we are required to live with a focus on our spiritual growth and betterment, striving to grow and learn in each future moment.

Fortunately, though seemingly difficult to resolve in theory, like almost all conflicts inherent in the divine mysteries of **One**, these conflicting positions work rather well together in action.

When you live in this moment, when you experience all that makes up the life around you, you charge up your spirit. So by making the most of *now*, you give energy to *later* that will assist you when *later* becomes *now*. It is truly that simple.

If each and every person who was looking for spiritual enlightenment to come to them focused on what is already around them now, they would find enlightenment easier and easier to see as each future moment became now. By experiencing the enlightenment in that moment of now, they would enrich themselves spiritually and be prepared to absorb even more from the next moment when it became now.

Soon, each moment of now would bring with it the powerful energy of enlightenment. There would be no more searching for what tomorrow will bring rather than looking at what now has to offer. Each person would develop an understanding that now is really the only place you are, so it is the only place that matters. Tomorrow will someday be now. If you have mastered now, you have mastered tomorrow.

Living in the moment, living now, is probably one of the most powerful tools you could develop to help you with your spiritual quest.

Living in One

Speaking about spiritual quests, in the last chapter we touched on another important aspect of **One** that we should revisit. That is the paradox that your spiritual quest is entirely your own and only you can get there by your own effort, yet you cannot do it alone and you need help with your effort.

Each person's effort to improve his or her own focus and understanding of what is helpful for the individual's unique spiritual quest is all that is actually needed to attain that spiritual goal. Regardless of how much assistance and information a person gleans from Teachers, Elders, Clerics, Spirit-guides, books, media, and any number of other outlets, the ultimate responsibility — and indeed the ultimate ability to absorb and utilize offered information — rest solely with the individual who is attempting to grow.

It has been wisely stated that no man (or woman) is an island. This also applies to each person's life in many ways including our spiritual ambitions. Although we can, as individuals, survive in our adult lives without assistance, in order to thrive in this life's journey we need the interactions of others.

Applying this to our spiritual life can be confusing. The divine mystery of **One** in this regard is clear. We must have help from others, yet we must make this sojourn totally alone. Paradoxical, nevertheless easily resolved.

The knowledge each of us needs in order to find our correct path can be elusive. Because few of us are privileged enough to live our lives solely for our spiritual objectives; and we each must deal with the rigors of maintaining a substance for ourselves and our families, few of us can devote one hundred percent of our time, thoughts, and energy to purely spiritual pursuits. Even those who are able to preserve their spiritual focus during the more mundane, everyday activities of life, cannot help but re-direct that focus at times when the mundane gives way to the unexpected. At these times, more noble efforts are set aside and coping with the problem at hand takes precedence.

In order to shelter those on the spiritual path from distractions — thus allowing these select individuals uninterrupted pursuit of spiritual enlightenment — it became customary in several cultures and religious orders to create areas of isolation where those considered pious were separated from the bulk of society.

Originally, it was believed that since the path to knowledge was walked from within, the distractions of everyday life would only derail and confound those who strived to bring spiritual enlightenment to the people. It was believed — and still is to this day in many places — that isolation from society and even separation from others who you share your isolation with, via such tools as a vow of celibacy or silence, give the individual the ability to devote every waking moment of their life to God and Heaven. In turn, the devotion of these people was intended to win favor with God for the community, thus making life for the common man better.

Did these select few individuals living in seclusion ever find the golden path to spiritual enlightenment? Did they ever find a secret door that led to the quick ascent to heaven? Did they ever discover their responsibility in the Universal Accord? If it were possible that they did, we would never truly know. Their seclusion also meant that they could not share what they learned.

So, just as it is conceivable that a unique species of plant or animal could evolve on a lone island out in the middle of the ocean, growing and thriving, yet be unknown to all the other creatures on the earth, it is also conceivable that some solitary soul, living a hermit's life in a remote monastery, discovered an easy, elusive, and direct path to the answers all humans seek. Unfortunately, just as the yet unknown new species is lost when the island sinks into the sea, the revelations of spiritual insights acquired by the devout recluse are lost when his body dies and his soul moves on.

That is, if it were possible that a solitary soul could attain such goals. It is not. The divine mystery of **One** which applies to spiritual growth clearly states that we need others to help us grow.

Even given the time to ponder the meaning of the universe, without distractions, without disruption, and without digression, each person can only go so far before they will come to something they cannot, do not, or will not understand.

Perhaps they cannot conceive of a truth because it is beyond their scope of intelligence as it is presented. The only way they can understand this truth and continue on the path is to have it explained to them by someone who understands it and can put it in more simple terms. Perhaps they do not conceive of a truth because it is so foreign to the current understand held by the individual that it does not seem to make sense. Therefore, they discard an important piece of the puzzle as being nonsense until such a time as interactions with others fosters an understanding that allows the person to see the value in the once discarded concept. Or, perhaps the truth offered challenges the individual to face something he or she does not wish to face, so he or she will not accept the truth. That is, not until another's words, actions, or energies provoke a confrontation of information and the person is driven to overcome the fear and attain understanding.

When we listen to others, when we learn from their words, they are not doing our work for us. By our willingness to absorb information, our efforts to comprehend that information, and most important, our discernment to judge if the information is worth anything to us, we work to better ourselves. It is not the information we have, but rather how much of that information we can effectively use that helps us grow.

Thus, by building on information given to us effectively and discretely, we alone make our spiritual journey. Only we, as individuals, can decide what we really believe. But with no one to give us their views — their roadmap to the cosmos — we would have no building material to begin with. The two are forever intertwined in a divine mystery of **One**.

This mystery also has another side. Remember the lone hermit in the monastery who shared his knowledge with no others. According to this mystery of **One**, he did no wrong by keeping what he learned to himself. To bring yourself along the path is all that is required of you. Nevertheless, paradoxically, he failed Creation's plan by not offering others the understanding he possessed. Arguably worse, he failed himself. For the greatest joy anyone can have in this life is assisting another to grow and reach their goal.

In our rush to find our spiritual direction, we may sometimes forget another divine mystery of **One** which we must hold onto every day. That is that the journey to creation is the reward for the trouble. Our prize for *getting there* is to have been allowed to make the journey. Taking time to enjoy the voyage, experiencing the companionship of other souls, opening many doors before finding the correct one, even making mistakes and getting hurt are all souvenirs we will hold forever of our travels.

How many of us rush to find the end of this path, hoping that a great reward awaits us? How many of us keep our focus so narrow and sharp that we see only straight ahead of us, as we rush headlong like warriors into battle, crushing the ground below our feet — often without regard. We struggle on as a fire in the wind. Our souls burn to reach our goal and claim our prize, never realizing that the prize is all around us. We look for a spiritual paradise where we are one with the Universal Accord, with God and creation, forgetting that the Universal Accord exists in all things, even earthly things. God and Creation are all around us — even in us.

Living in **One** requires that we remember Creation and the Creator are not separate things. The Creator is an individual. The Creator is that which became — the Thought, the Word. The Creator is the only one. The Creator is that which came first. The Creator is what which will be last, for it will still be there when everything it created is gone. The Creator is as individual and unique as anything could ever be. Yet, that which the Creator has made, that being creation, is truly unified with the Creator. It is not unified as a man and a woman are. It is not that the Creator is one thing and creation is another. The Creator and what the Creator has made are the same exact thing.

There is nothing that exists outside of creation. For everything that exists, in both physical and non-physical places are part of creation. If the truth be known, there is no *outside* to creation. There is only an *inside* to creation. All things are inside creation. Everything, everywhere, in all times, spaces, and realities, understood and not understood by any and all awarenesses are included in

Living in One

creation. We know this because we know that all things come from the Creator. If there was anything outside of this creation, it too would have to have been created by the Creator, and by default would become part of the Creator's creation. Since there can be nothing beyond creation, without it becoming creation, it is only logical to conclude that the Creator is also part of creation. The paradox of the divine mystery of **One** here is clear and can be summed up in one of two questions:

The first question could be; if the Creator is part of the creation yet made all of creation, did the Creator somehow become when creation began?

Secondly, if you see it from the other side of the coin, you may ask; if there is nothing beyond creation and all that exists is part of this creation, is their truly a Creator?

The answer to these questions have beleaguered many a scholar for many generations. But if you consider the divine mystery of **One**, and understand the paradoxical nature of it, you will be able to accept the following truth. The Creator and that which is created are the same, yet different. The Creator is the energy of understanding, the master plan, the Universal Accord that controls the movement and growth of creation. Creation is the energy that is put into motion by that master plan — the energy of thought and action. Just as you think, then do, so does Creation and the Creator.

This is not a new concept and has been understood for many, many generations. Even as far back as biblical times we can see the concept. The Bible tells us in John 1:1 **In the beginning was the Word, and the Word was WITH God, and the Word WAS God.**

As you can see, in the beginning was the word. The word is thought, inspiration, realization, consciousness, self-awareness. The Creator dared to think the thought that started it all and Creation came into being. That thought — that word — was with the Creator. That thought — that word — was the Creator. Thus, we can see, Creation and the Creator are both with each other, and the same as each other. The paradox. They are uniquely different things, yet they are the same thing.

Living in One

This is an important thing to keep in mind, especially when you consider that you are a part of creation.

Moreover, this divine mystery of **One** does not stop with the Creator. It also applies to individual life forms here on Earth. Notice I did not say people. It is because everything that has consciousness is subjected to this rule of **One**, not just humans.

Because creation and the Creator are the same thing, and because all things in creation are made from the eternal energy that makes up both Creator and creation, additionally because this energy is eternal in all directions, not just in the way of time unending, all conscious beings are not only totally unique — as each individual has their own experience, focus and perspective — each individual is exactly the same as all pieces of creation's energy, regardless of what forms those pieces take in the physical world.

What this means, in relation to your place in the Universal Accord, is that you are no more or less important than anything or anyone else in creation. This considered, your place in execution of the Universal Accord will be quite different from that of any other person, or thing you are likely to encounter. Your job may be far more important than that of a bumblebee in the overall scheme of things. On the same token, your job may be far less important than that of an Angel or Spiritual Guide. But who is to say. Perhaps, without the occupants of Earth ever knowing it, the actions of one lone bumblebee has changed the course of human-kind's evolution far more than anyone born in a human body ever has.

That each person is unique is not hard for most of us to understand. That we are all exactly the same in an energy sense is more difficult. People, in general, strive to make a name for themselves. People struggle for a unique identity that separates them from the crowd. People pride themselves on what makes them different as a race, culture, and individual. It is no wonder the concept of all living things — including animals, bugs, plants, and trees — having identical energy is difficult for many to feel comfortable with.

Living in One

Many cultures from human-kind's past had a basic understanding of this. Often, with the advent of what could be called sophisticated ideologies, the understanding of the unique yet identical energies of non-human living things on planet Earth was lost. Recognizing and acknowledging the different brother/sister energies possessed by the other creatures of Earth was misinterpreted by those who considered themselves educated and civilized as polytheism and a threat to their monotheistic imperial ways. Over time, with persistence and ridicule, much of the understanding of the different energies inherent in other living creatures of Earth was lost. Few today understand it. Even many who follow in traditional ways do not understand the depth of what it means to commune with the spirit of Brother Bear or the essence of Sister Eagle. It is not that we are connected to these other occupants of Earth because we share a like energy. It is because we are the exact same energy. We are identical in the concept of **One**.

Returning to the concept of polytheism for a moment, it has been expounded by many theologies that society will progress though the ignorance of polytheism, to eventually discover the unity of one powerful source of universal understanding — one God. This is yet another narrow view of the cosmos that must be challenged if you live in **One**.

The paradoxical nature of reality demands that both concepts of monotheism and polytheism exist in harmony together to explain the very same Creator. How? As established already, the Creator and creation are not just with other, they are each other. So, to look at the Creator as being the one who created and creation the separate thing that was created, we see that the universal order is a monotheistic structure. There is only one force to the universe. The Creator made all things.

Yet, if we look at the Creator in unity with what is created — if we look from the perspective that is represented in the phrase, *the Word was God,* we can extrapolate the following as we examine the parts of the creation: The first thing to remember in this perspective is that the Creator is part of the creation. All things in creation are identical in respect to the energy that makes them. Accordingly, all things in creation are identical to that which created them. Thus,

Living in One

there are many, many countenances of the Creation force around you in the world today. All things in creation are a manifestation of that which created them. All things created are countless faces of one God energy. This is true polytheism in its purest form.

To live in **One** is to live with and come to accept all the paradoxes **One** encompasses. For example, Polytheism versus monotheism — or more properly stated, polytheism is monotheism — is a divine mystery of **One**.

All parts of creation are identical energy to that which created them. Everything around you is a part of God. All energies are God. There is no separation. When this is understood, we can see that there are an infinite number of Gods, Creators, and Spirits. Even our own souls qualify as one of these things, if not all of them. Many Gods equals polytheism. Yet, there is only one creation, and thus, one Creator — one God. Monotheism.

This may be a difficult concept for some to come into agreement with. After all, it is a paradox and it does bring with it a vast amount of responsibility. To sincerely understand beyond a shadow of a doubt that you are more than just one with the Creator and one with creation, but that you are actually a parallel awareness of God, brings with it more than just a feeling of belonging. It is only when you truly understand that you are not only with God, but you are God, that you understand the importance of everything you do.

Moreover, when you come to understand that everything around, every person, animal, river, mountain, star, and insect is also an equivalent parallel awareness of the God that you are, your responsibility becomes even greater.

When we are forced to realize that everything is made from the energy that is the Creator, not separate from the creator, we find we must reassess our actions in relationship to the world around us. You may assume that this responsibility is limited to becoming responsible for the way we abuse the planet's eco system, and perhaps people around us. But there is more.

Once we realize and come to be aware of the energy of the Creator in all things, we come to understand that the feeling we had that day when we stood on the hillside and the wind blew through our hair and filled our hearts with a calm, yet stimulating sense of the eternal, was not just the friction of the wind blowing over the nerve endings in our skin, but it was the energy of the wind, the Creator in the wind. It was the life-force of the wind. In other words, it was the very alive, very real, spirit of the wind. It is a spirit just as alive as that which lights our own souls, although the form it takes is different. Its energy is an identical fractal of creation to our own. It is exactly the same as each of us is in the tapestry which is the Creator — God.

That there is a spirit to the wind may not be a hard concept for you to accept. It is more likely you will find it harder to believe that the wind could have a soul. It is an odd thing that when we feel energy in something such as wind, water, or rocks, we can accept that there is an energy and even a spirit to the thing, yet we cannot seem to go as far as to believe there is a soul to the thing. Could this be because to accept something such as the wind has a soul, we must accept that it has something we often reserve only for ourselves and those few special animals in

One: Discovering the True Nature of The Universal Accord

our lives? Could it be that we cannot believe the wind has a soul because it would mean that the wind has sentience?

Sentience is something we as human beings tend to reserve for ourselves only. We justify everything we do on planet earth, and do to planet earth, by convincing ourselves that we are the only things on earth that are sentient. Once in a while, we may go as far as to accept that our pets are sentient. We convince ourselves that our dogs and cats have souls, awareness, and understanding, but cows and chickens do not. After all, if we believed that chickens could love the way our dear pet could, then we would have to face a moral dilemma each time we wanted to have dinner.

This behavior of selective identification of sentience is a protective device that mankind collectively invented after turning his back on what was considered primitive, polytheistic thinking. By holding the belief that only humans have sentience, humans give themselves a carte blanche of sorts that allows them to do as they wish with all other things on the planet.

Living in One

Unlike those they labeled primitive, polytheistic, earth-based, savages, they disregard the importance of keeping the balance of the divine mystery of **One** that says, "Though there is only one Creator and one Creation, there are infinite manifestations of that one Creator in the Creation."

By inventing the belief that all things were created solely for human consumption without responsibility or compensation, people came to believe that they negated their responsibility to these energies as they used them up.

By ignoring the energies, humans felt justified as they clear-cut forests, fouled rivers and lakes, and killed animal species until they were endangered or extinct. It was not until their ecological transgressions became a problem for people, that the human race stopped to think about what they were doing to the world. It was not until the game animals were so scarce that there was barely anything left to hunt that hunting for sport became regulated to certain seasons and locations. It was not until fish were so few and small that the fishing industry started to loose profits, that trolling with huge nets and cleaning whole breeding beds of fish was regulated. It was not until the air was so foul with smoke and soot that people began to die, that regulations were put on factories.

So, it was not until the balance of **One** was so far out of equilibrium that it caused severe physical consequences did mankind stand up and take notice.

Unfortunately, the efforts made by most people to try and re-order this balance are not because they understand the **One** that is effected, but rather, simply because they know something needs to be fixed before they are subjected to worse discomfort. The changes they make are in a direction that is appropriate, but are not being made for the proper reasons.

Perhaps, once the effort to balance the environment is made, the power of **One** that will come into balance will infuse the people with the truth they are restoring with their efforts.

In addition to ecological efforts to conserve and restore the environment, there are other things each of us can do to re-

Living in One

establish our connection to the energies of **One** in our life. We should always take the time to be mindful of the energies that go into our food and the products we use. It would do us all some good if each of us took a moment to acknowledge the universal creation energy that gave its earth existence for our sustenance that is in that chicken leg and broccoli on our dinner plate. We should be mindful of the energies that go into the creation of the things around us. Even plastic and other substances that are not natural to the earth come from things that are natural to the earth. They are still made from the bits that are physical forms of the energy of creation. In this basic way, you and your computer are more alike than you may wish to believe.

Also, we all should be mindful that everything created by anything with self awareness holds the essence of the being that created it. That is why there is such energy in music, art and dance. These things are obvious. The same can be said for technology, textiles, and simple basic things such as your comb, toothbrush, and shoes. These things may have been invented so long ago and are so common that you do not take the time to realize the genius and energy that went into their creation. But the energy is still there because energy is eternal.

To live in **One** is to understand that everything you do effects the greater creation you are one with. This compels each of us to do the best we can for ourselves, yet at the same time do the best we can for those around us and our world. Sometimes what we perceive as best for ourselves as individuals is not what we know is best for the others around us, or the world in which we all live. At these times, we might feel we are facing the concept of **Two** or even **Three** as we try to balance seemingly different goals with either equality or a middle ground. But if we can remove the physical aspects from these situations and look at the greater spiritual questions involved, we will be able to understand the focus of the **One** involved and we should be able to resolve the issue — that is, if we truly wish to.

Sometimes the resolution of issues concerning **One** force us to choose that which is self-sacrificing before that which is pleasant. It can often be difficult to choose the noble path over and over again, ignoring what you want from the perspective of a physical being who needs physical comforts. Though, over time, we each will find that giving into the wishes of the Universal Accord, rather than our cardinal physical needs, will payoff in ways we cannot begin to imagine if we look at it from a corporal perspective.

To live in **One** is to understand that you are a working part of the Universal Accord, and that by your very existence here on earth you inherit certain responsibilities to assist the Universal Accord in its objectives. To live in **One** is to realize that there is truly only ONE thing in this cosmos and beyond. That one thing is all encompassing, including all things physical and non-physical in nature. Or, you could say, it is both matter and energy. In fact, matter is simply energy in a different form. Again, what seems like a balance of two things is really the same one thing from a different perspective.

Consider the following paradox of **One**: The Universal Accord can be called the blueprint that controls the development of creative energy in the universe around you. This creates the supposition that all things are preordained to a previously scripted plan. Yet, energy is random and the details of any growth situation must remain unknown to the greater energy experiencing and learning from it, or there would be no value to the lesson presented. Thus, regardless of the plan's existence, those who are working out the details of that plan cannot fully know what will unfold, less they lose the opportunity to add knowledge and experience to the Universal Accord.

Confusing? Perhaps so. But what it means for people in the physical universe is simple. It means that even though you may be able to see where you are going in the end, the path you choose and the path you actually travel to get there are likely to be very different.

This is as it should be. For even though you are destined to do a certain job, or accomplish a certain mission in this life, the way you do it is going to be something left to be discovered. It will involve agreements, emotions, relationships, and new experiences that will all create twists and turns in your path that are too numerous to plot ahead of time. These sudden changes, discoveries, and forks in the road you choose, create the dynamics of life.

Living in One

Your life must hold an element of indeterminateness so that you are given opportunities to make choices, and learn from those choices. Thus, you add your experience to that of the Universal Accord.

CHAPTER EIGHT
THE UNIVERSAL ACCORD

The plan of creation. The blue print of the unfolding of time. The plot to the eternal performance. The meaning of life. Many words have been used to try to describe the Universal Accord.

As you learn to recognize the forces of **Three**, **Two,** and **One** in your life, and you begin to see the power of the divine mysteries of **One** working in all things around you, you will begin to regain your connection to the Universal Accord from which you came.

The Universal Accord is more than simply an agreed upon plan of Creation. It is the place where this plan is unfolding. It is the time when the plan is being executed. It is the life that is carrying out the plan. It is being implemented in heaven, earth, and every place else. Its plan unfolds each time you escape the muddy middle ground of a **Three**, and its strategy is tested every time you find the balance of the opposing **Two**. But most importantly, every moment you live in **One**, you strengthen the resolve of the Universal Accord to create a positive future unfolding in the physical cosmos for all who exist in it.

It is important to remember that every individual, including yourself — especially yourself — has a responsibility to make the best of his or her lifetime. Each one of us has the duty to learn to understand the different energies in our life, thus understand what drives us to do what we do. We each much strive to live in **One** so that we can be a working part of the Universal Accord — the agreement with God we committed to upon our creation in physical form. Each and every one of us needs to understand that the Universal Accord is not some faraway concept that we can imagine, but do little about. The Universal Accord is the design we all agreed to live and work by.

It is the thread that binds all things in a divine and complex dance of creation. It is the energy that makes up all souls and the fire that burns in all living things to continue. It is yours. It is mine. It belongs to all things, all beings, everywhere.

There is nothing that is not a part of the Universal Accord. Even things evil, dark, and hurtful are part of the plan. Every movie has to have a villain or there can be no hero. Even the story of the unfolding of the consciousness of Creation has to have some kind of villain so the hero can have something to triumph over.

The concepts of **Three**, **Two,** and **One** are at work every moment in the revealing motions of the eternal clockwork, just as they are working every day in your own life. For you are a micro-reflection, like a fractal of the greater whole of the Universal Accord itself. Because of this, the greater and more whole you make your life, the greater and more whole the gift you bring back to Creation will be.

Take a moment to think of the Universal Accord as a book full of chapters that make the story. Turn to the chapter

The Universal Accord

about you! Are the pages blank? You hold the pen. Write your story! Make it as wonderful and fulfilling as you possibly can. It is *your* life. It is *your* chapter. This is **YOUR** chance to make a difference in the plan of creation.

You are not just following a plan, you are writing that plan as you go. Your life, your freewill choices, and your actions and reactions to people and things around you is your chapter in this book. It is your contribution to Creation itself. And although it is all the following things, the Universal Accord is more than just a God or Gods making decisions and creating friction. It is more than some impossibly large narrative of the history of consciousness through the ages. It is even more than the true source of life and awareness. The Universal Accord is more than heaven's blueprints.

The Universal Accord becomes alive in your heart when you open your heart to the energy of God. It is more than something outside yourself. It is inside you. It is what you are. The Universal Accord is YOU when you live in **ONE**. This is the true nature of the Universal Accord. ଔ

www.ingramcontent.com/pod-product-compliance
Lightning Source LLC
LaVergne TN
LVHW041628070426
835507LV00008B/505

9 780974 543444